The Fast Way to Power

DR SHAUN MARLER

The Fast Way to Power
by Dr. Shaun Marler

Published by:
World Harvest Ministries, PO Box 90, Bald Hills, Qld, 4036, Australia
www.whm.org.au

This book or parts thereof may not be reproduced in any form, stored in a retrieval system, or transmitted in any form, by any means - electronic, mechanical, photocopy, recording or otherwise - without prior written permission of the author or publisher, except as provided by Australian copyright law.

All scriptural references are taken from the King James Bible unless otherwise stated.

Cover Design by Sarah Freeman

Copyright © Shaun Marler 2022

First Published June 2022

ISBN: 978-0-6450609-2-8

This Book is Dedicated to the Extension of the Kingdom of God.

This book is dedicated to you the believer, the person who desires and hungers to know Christ more and the power of His resurrection. To the ones who want to see revival in their lives and ministries. It is my sincere prayer that what is contained in this book will be a real help and blessing to you, empowering you to win in life through Jesus Christ.

I pray this revelation, 'The Fast Way to Power' and the importance of living a fasted life, will help you to walk in what the early saints of old walked and lived in.

It will assist you to take another step into the glory of God, as you allow the Holy Spirit to reveal these truths to your mind and spirit. Imparting their power and importance from the Son of God to your heart.

Love in Jesus,
Pastor Shaun

Foreword

I first met Pastor Shaun Marler when he was 19 years of age. I was leading Christian Outreach Centre. He received the baptism of the Holy Spirit that night.

Pastor Shaun began living in a new dimension of Spirit life, as I did when I received the baptism of the Holy Spirit.

This experience lifts each of us into a new realm of life, where miracles happen, where you are empowered by God to do the works of Christ. I believe through the scriptures and personal experience that it is essential to receive this experience.

I came from being a stockman in the Northern Territory, on a million acre property which was remote and came south to manage another property. I went to a Billy Graham crusade meeting where I gave my life to Christ.

The salvation experience was beyond life transforming to me. Like millions of other people, it was the start of my spiritual walk not the climax. It was a long journey and I gradually learned to find my spiritual feet as it were. If you find it difficult to maintain a life in the Spirit, don't give up, and as you learn from the bible and others, your life settles into a spiritual rhythm, the Holy Spirit carries you when you cannot carry yourself. I have seen large numbers of people come to Christ and thousands of people healed by the power of the Holy Spirit of all types of sickness and disease. In the beginning, the healings were just enough to keep me going on the journey of the Spirit-led life .

I saw a man moving in the gift of the word of knowledge. I watched with awe as God revealed hidden things about the man and as he prayed, the man was healed. It was an amazing night and continued for some hours. As I watched, a great hunger to see the Holy Spirit work through my life was more than birthed in me I was consumed with this longing to help people with all sorts of sickness, disease and problems.

You cannot do these things in your human ability, you have to know God is in you, that you can rely on Him to flow through you and heal or deliver as the person needs.

It is when you stand before large or small numbers of people and you know that you in your humanity cannot supply what they need. Only God can do that. It is then you feel your utter lack and I knew that I had to rely absolutely on the Holy Spirit.

For one year I longed for the Holy Spirit to move through me and I think I fasted more than I ate that year . I wanted to see God move more than I wanted food. I found that fasting made me more sensitive to the things of the Spirit. By the end of the year my spirit was sensitised to the Holy Spirit and I could hear Him speak with clarity.

In this book, Pastor Shaun covers the subject of fasting thoroughly. Both scripturally and he tells the story of many of the greats in church history. You will be brought to a point of decision, what will I do with this biblical subject of fasting?

To me the great benefit, of fasting is that:
1. You put seeking Gods will above your human need for food. It demonstrates your desire for the things of God more than your daily bread.
2. You become sensitised to the still whisper of God within.
3. Your spirit gains ascendency and you are more open to the realm of the spirit.

I trust that as you read this book, it will bring you to your need for a closer walk with God. If so, your life will be richer, more satisfying, an inner peace will pervade you and any price you paid will be as nothing to all you have gained.

May God open the eyes of your spirit as you read this book.

Pastor Clark Taylor

But as truly as I live, all the earth shall be filled with the glory of the Lord.

-Numbers 14:21-

Arise, shine; for thy light is come, and the glory of the Lord is risen upon thee.

For, behold, the darkness shall cover the earth, and gross darkness the people: but the Lord shall arise upon thee, and his glory shall be seen upon thee.

And the Gentiles shall come to thy light, and kings to the brightness of thy rising.

-Isaiah 60:1-3-

**If you want something
you have never had,
you have to do something
you have never done!**

-Shaun Marler-

Acknowledgements

I would like to acknowledge my good friends Drummond R. Thom and Don Gossett, who are now promoted to the presence of the Lord, for all their help and input over the years that I knew them.

For the numerous occasions I have been able to glean from their knowledge of the Word and experience in ministry of these men of God. To hear these men share about the great men and women of God that they have personally worked with and known. To ask about their prayer lives. Learning the secrets of fasting and prayer. You find out that many of the great healing evangelists were men and women who prayed earnestly and fasted for the power and presence of God.

Thank You

I would like to thank my wife Kerrie, and family for their understanding of and supporting me in the ministry. A big thank you to Pastor Brian Hicks for always supporting and believing in me. I would also like to thank the faithful members of my church congregation at World Harvest Ministries, Bald Hills, to whom I have had the great joy and privilege of sharing God's Word, now for over forty years. You know who you are. Thank you for believing in me, encouraging me, drawing out of me the good Word of God and revelations (kisses from the Father) that I have received over the years.

You have inspired me to press in, to keep on studying, learning more and teaching you, your children and others, what I have learned and received from our Lord.

Plus a big thank you to Tony and Jeanie Stone, and Evangelist Steve Ryder, from whom I learnt how to operate in God's miracle ministry. You have all helped me prepare and bring this book to print.

You will always be in my heart.

Contents

Introduction 19

Chapter One WHY, WHEREFORE, HOW 23

Chapter Two THE ABC'S OF REVIVAL 33

Chapter Three THE CURE FOR UNBELIEF 55

Chapter Four THE IMPORTANCE OF FASTING 61

Chapter Five RESULTS OF FASTING 73

Chapter Six PROBLEM, ACTION, ANSWER 91

Chapter Seven DANIEL INTERCEDES ON BEHALF OF ISRAEL 97

Chapter Eight FASTING SUPERCHARGES PRAYER 111

Chapter Nine A TWENTY-THREE DAY FAST FOR REVIVAL 137

Chapter Ten SEVEN BASIC STEPS TO SUCCESSFUL FASTING & PRAYER 149

Chapter Eleven HOW TO EXPERIENCE AND MAINTAIN PERSONAL REVIVAL 157

Chapter Twelve A CLARION CALL 159

Appendix 176

Footnotes 189

THE FAST WAY TO POWER

FAST WAY TO POWER

INTRODUCTION

This book is not for every *Believer*, though every *Believer* should read this book. This book is written for the *Believer* who desires to see and live in God's miracle power and the Revival Life! The *Believer* who desires more of God's power, more of God's goodness, more of God's presence.

It is for the *Believer* who is sick and tired, of being sick and tired and broke. The one who wants to experience the reality of God and His power found in the Bible. This book contains the secret to the fast way, to that power!

The purpose of fasting is not to lose weight. The purpose is to seek the face of God, to draw closer to Him and to have a revelation of His will for your life. As you do this, you will find many other benefits. You will find the anointing and power of God moving in your life, you will see the yokes of bondage broken, and your health restored.

Fasting and prayer are the keys to a mature, rich and rewarding life in the Spirit, and fulfilment in your life as you walk with God.

If you want what God has, you have to be willing to do a little self denying.

• Noah died to self. For 120 years he built a boat all because God told him to. (Genesis 6).

• Paul became the Apostle to the Gentiles, but before this happened, he first had to die to self. We read that he went into the desert for three years alone with God.

• Charles Finney carried an unusual anointing. As he approached the outskirts of a town, we read that nearly the whole town would fall on their knees to repent. Why did God use him above others of his day? Because he had died to self.

• Smith Wigglesworth was used to perform many miracles. It is stated that he raised 29 people from the dead. Why did God use this man? Because he had died to self.

If we again look at the life of Charles Finney we will see what he has to say on this subject of dying to self, he says: "Thoroughly examine the state of your heart and see where you are. Check to see if you are walking with God every day or with the devil."

• We must examine our life
    o   Does known sin exist?
    o   Have we dealt with the sin in our lives?
    o   What controls our lives, is it God, or is it flesh?

• Examine your love for God
    o   What is the first love of your life?

o How much time do you spend in prayer every day?
o What place does God's Word hold in your life?

Prayer and fasting were part of the daily life of Jesus. We are instructed in the Word to follow the example that He has set. Jesus said His disciples would fast often.

There are some people who study history, while others make it. I want to be part of the latter group.

If we want what the early disciples had, we have to do what they did.

Fasting is important because God has ordained it in His Word.

Fasting is an important part of self-denial or denial of the flesh.

One of the strongest desires of the flesh is food. It is during a fast that one denies himself food.

But remember the idea is to live a stronger Christian life, not to die, so always use wisdom in your fasting and seek medical advice before going on long periods of fasting. Where practically possible, inform a mentor, pastor or mature Christian leader of your fast. They will be able to pray for you and monitor your progress during this time, stay accountable to a peer.

In writing this book, it is my desire, that your time spent in fasting and prayer is successful, effective and productive.

It is not to be a one time event but a discipline you add to your Christian walk that leads to an increase of God's manifest power in your life. Resulting in answered prayer and a deeper, stronger relationship with your God.

Chapter One

WHY, WHEREFORE, HOW

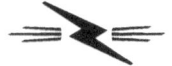

Before we begin fasting, it is wise to arm ourselves with some information on the subject. I hope that by the time you have finished reading this book, you will be excited and inspired with a new zeal and understanding on the powerful revelation of the discipline of fasting, the results you can expect to achieve, and the things you can expect to face during your fast.

In Matthew chapter six, Jesus outlines the three main disciplines of the Christian faith, Praying, Giving & Fasting.

Why

To be a disciple of Jesus Christ, we should be disciplined followers of Him and His teachings. As James 1: 22 says, *"But be ye doers of the word, and not hearers only, deceiving your own selves."*

Delayed Gratification

Discipline is delayed gratification. Any elite athlete will tell you, to be an Olympian it is going to take a lot of discipline to their chosen field of endeavour. An Olympic swimmer will be up before the break of day and in the pool doing their laps while their friends sleep in after late nights out. Not so for the elite athlete, they have to discipline their time, their diet, their sleep regime and their whole way of life in order to achieve that Olympic medal. They have to delay the gratification of their flesh and social activities and social life in so many ways.

The apostle Paul speaks about this in 1 Corinthians 9:25-26, how like a fine athlete, he keeps his body disciplined to achieve gold for God.

> *"Everyone who competes in the games goes into strict training. They do it to get a crown that will not last, but we do it to get a crown that will last forever. Therefore I do not run like someone running aimlessly; I do not fight like a boxer beating the air"* (1 Corinthians 9:25-26 NIV).

We can see here that Paul is referring to discipline, the strict training that athletes put themselves through in order to win gold. An athlete will prepare physically mentally and emotionally. This will include their exercise regime, dietary requirements, sleep and mental preparation etc. A highly trained athlete will go through a lot of delayed gratification. Self pleasures and time, in order to achieve their goals.

As a disciple, disciplined follower of Christ, we will at times and in various ways have to delay our own gratification for the greater benefit of the body of Christ. Jesus taught us to pray in Matthew 6:9-13, not our will but God's will be done in our life.

> *"After this manner therefore pray ye: Our Father which art in heaven, Hallowed be thy name. Thy kingdom come, Thy will be done in earth, as it is in heaven. Give us this day our daily bread. And forgive us our debts, as we forgive our debtors. And lead us not into temptation, but deliver us from evil: For thine is the kingdom, and the power, and the glory, for ever. Amen"* (Matthew 6:9-13).

History Makers

The call of God, the purposes of heaven and seeking first His kingdom and His righteousness must be first place in our lives.

Wherefore

In 1 Corinthians 7:5, it speaks of where a husband and a wife can delay their gratification of sexual and physical relations to give themselves to a time of prayer and fasting.

> Amos 3.3 says, *"..how can two walk together except they be agreed."*

It is a mutually agreed upon time of consecration to devote themselves to greater intimacy with God, which eventually results in deeper intimacy with each other. Then as outlined in the Word, they come back together again (sexually) so that Satan doesn't tempt them to look outside the relationship for gratification (sex). I will touch on the disciplines of prayer and giving in this book, but my main concern in writing this book is the lack and greatly neglected discipline of fasting in the body of Christ, as taught by Jesus.

Fasting could possibly be the most neglected Christian discipline in the modern-day church, where we have been so blessed by the great benefits, blessings and freedoms that Christianity has brought to our world. I believe that we Christians will see greater results as we supercharge our prayers and giving with fasting. The revivals that we long to see will break forth as a result of this new hunger for God. Through fasting, we discipline our flesh bringing it under the submission to the Spirit. We allow the Spirit to reign in us; we humble our flesh and allow God to exalt us.

How

Now, are you ready to embark on an exciting journey with me to learn about how to release the incredible and life-changing power of God through the discipline of fasting!

Get ready to receive new insight, revelation knowledge and fine tune your spiritual ears to hear from God as never before. This will ultimately build the Kingdom of God in your sphere of influence as you see His Kingdom come, and His will done in your life to a greater degree. Strongholds will be pulled down which will strengthen your Christian walk, your love and devotion to God and your faith will increase as you pray to see the great harvest of souls promised the church in these last days.

Through *'The Fast Way to Power'*, the *Believer* will be equipped to help harvest the billion of souls, that have been prophesied to come into the Kingdom of God through the last great revival before Jesus comes.

The following extract is taken from an article, I read once, written by a doctor for a health farm retreat.

Why Fast?

1. More is scientifically known about fasting than any other natural alternative healing technique.
2. Fasting, in many ways, plays an important role in spiritual growth and awareness.
3. It is a discipline in every major religion.
4. Fasting is a natural way of healing the body.
5. The healthiest people on earth fast regularly.
6. Fasting is the least toxic and least expensive therapy.
7. Fasting is simple.
8. The human body is biologically designed to fast.
9. Fasting is a personal education and self-awareness process.
10. Fasting builds the systemic health of the whole body.
11. The optimum results are obtained by regular fasting.

Now, these are some excellent reasons to fast, wouldn't you say!

But now let's have a look at what God's Word has to say on the subject, and I am sure you will be so motivated and excited, that you will not be able to wait to begin your next fast.

"Faith begins where the will of God is known." I first heard this statement in Bible College listening to Brother Kenneth Hagin on videotape. Something went off on the inside of me, and from that day, I have had a great desire to know, understand and live in God's will for my life. When I was a young man of nineteen, God challenged my heart to make a fresh commitment of my life to Him. At that time we lived on a small farm, it was slightly raining, and in the early evening light, I went down the back paddock, knelt down on the ground and prayed a simple prayer of consecration and dedication of my life to God.

I told God I would do a deal with Him. I would give Him my whole heart; live my whole life for Him on the condition that He would give me everything He had. Little did I know then, but that was exactly what God had done already for all of His children. He had already sent Jesus to die for us, given us Sonship through Him, made us a joint-heir of all that He has and wants to freely give us all things with Jesus. (Romans 8:14-17).

I can testify since that day I have travelled to more than thirty nations of the world to date. I have had the privilege of praying for countless thousands of people, seeing hundreds of thousands saved, healed and baptised in the Holy Ghost by the power of God through my simple prayers of faith.

The deaf have heard, the blind have seen, the dumb have spoken, cripples have been made whole, and the captives set free. To this day, people still receive divine healing from God and relief from pain, as I pray and give simple commands in the mighty name of Jesus Christ of Nazareth.

Many times when I have had my back to the wall, been caught between a rock and a hard place, I have set aside a time to fast and through that time of seeking the Lord and discipline of fasting, God has broken me into a new level of answered prayer and victory.

God's Word will inspire you to reach out and take back from the hand of the enemy what he has stolen from you.

Now one last thing, before we begin our journey into fasting.

- If you have never fasted before, go slow! No extended fast should be undertaken without first getting advice from your physician.
- You can start fasting by just missing one meal and work your way up to a whole day.
- Remember always drink plenty of water while you fast.
- Call on the Holy Spirit, He will lead, guide and strengthen you.

AND REMEMBER, JESUS SAID MY DISCIPLES WILL FAST OFTEN. Luke 5:33-35

If we are going to be disciples or disciplined followers of Jesus:
- We need to read the Word daily and do it.
- We need to pray continually.
- We need to tithe and give offerings.
- We need to let our mouth be full of God's praise and thanksgiving.

- We need to establish a regular habit of fasting as led by the Spirit of God. This will ensure that we walk in the VICTORY, we have in Jesus Christ.

Jesus taught that you could supercharge your prayer life by fasting. Mark 9:23-29.

"Jesus said unto him, If thou canst believe, all things are possible to him that believeth. And straightway the father of the child cried out, and said with tears, Lord, I believe; help thou mine unbelief. When Jesus saw that the people came running together, he rebuked the foul spirit, saying unto him, Thou dumb and deaf spirit, I charge thee, come out of him, and enter no more into him. And the spirit cried, and rent him sore, and came out of him: and he was as one dead; insomuch that many said, He is dead. But Jesus took him by the hand, and lifted him up; and he arose. And when he was come into the house, his disciples asked him privately, Why could not we cast him out? And he said unto them, This kind can come forth by nothing, but by prayer and fasting" (Mark 9:23-29).

I believe the power of fasting as it relates to prayer is the spiritual nuclear bomb that our Lord has given to us, to destroy the strongholds of evil and usher in the last great revival and spiritual harvest around the world.

The Call

God is calling us to fast, and He would not make such a call without a specific reason or purpose.

Our confidence is in the Lord to help us. The Holy Spirit will refresh our soul and spirit. Our faith will soar as we humble ourselves and cry out to God and soak while we rejoice in His presence.

A divine visit from heaven will kindle the greatest spiritual harvest in the history of the Church. But before God comes in revival power, the Holy Spirit will call millions of God's people to repent, fast, and pray in the spirit of 2 Chronicles 7:14:

> *"If my people, who are called by my name, will humble themselves and pray and seek my face and turn from their wicked ways, then I will hear from heaven and will forgive their sin and will heal their land."*

I believe that as we fast and pray, two worlds will collide, heaven and earth, the spiritual man and the carnal man. The carnal man will yield to the spiritual man and heaven will invade earth by first invading the earthen vessels of our heart.

The scope of this revival depends on how believers in Australia and the rest of the world respond to this call to fast and pray.

Chapter Two

THE ABC'S OF REVIVAL

One day I asked my good friend Don Gossett, if he could tell me what the secret was to the power and ministry of some of the great men and women of God, that he had the privilege, honour and pleasure of working with, in his life. Don Gossett was a mighty man of God, a true "Father in the Faith" and wrote more than 120 books, plus many other pamphlets, tracts, poems and pieces of literature. Don, who is now in heaven with Jesus, was in the full-time ministry for six or more decades. During which time, he fellowshipped with some of the people we now call God's Great Generals. Don had personally known and ministered with the likes of William Branham, Kathryn Kulhman, William Freeman, Raymond T. Richey, Oral Roberts, the Jeffries brothers, Gordon Lindsay, T. L. Osborn and the list goes on. Don Gossett travelled first hand, with some of these men that literally turned the world upside down with their faith.

I also asked Don, "Tell me, what did you observe to be the secret of their power and presence of God?" What Don said to me I will never forget, and I will share it with you as keys to "stepping into the supernatural". Don told me something that was very simple yet very profound. He said, "Well Shaun, they knew their ABC's." I said, "What do you mean, Don; they knew their ABC's? Please explain what are the ABC's?" He said, "Shaun, 'A' stands for Authority, 'B' for Boldness and 'C' for Compassion." He then explained to me, how in the lives of these great men and women that had worked powerful miracles for the Lord and wrought wonders by faith and had led many souls to Jesus.

These men and women knew their authority in Christ; they knew who they were in Christ and who Christ was in them. They knew the power and authority of the Name of Jesus. They knew that at that Name, every knee must bow and every tongue confess that Jesus Christ is Lord, to the glory of God the Father. They knew that all authority, both in Heaven and in the earth, had been delivered unto Jesus. They had been sent forth by Him in the power of that authority, to make disciples of all men, heal the sick, destroy the works of the devil and establish the Kingdom of God.

These men and women were BOLD. They were FEARLESS in the face of the enemy. They were FEARLESS in the face of man. They were FEARLESS regardless of how hard, impossible, difficult or grave the circumstance at hand. They knew that greater was He that is in them than he that is in the world. They knew that God had not given them a spirit of fear, but He had given them a spirit of love, power and a sound mind. They knew that perfect love casteth out ALL fear. They knew that they were righteous, born again, born to win, born to overcome, more than conquerors through Him who loved them. They knew that Jesus, who knew no sin, had become sin for them, that they might be made the righteousness of God in Christ. They knew that they were new creations and that they were called to reign and rule in life through Jesus Christ. They knew that they could do all things through Christ who strengthens them.

They knew that nothing was impossible for their God and that all things are possible to them that believe! They knew the righteous are as bold as lions and that their righteousness was of God. They had put on the whole armour of God, and they wore by faith the breastplate of righteousness. By faith, they stood in the grace (unmerited favour of God that would divinely enable them to succeed in whatever they put their hand unto) and this knowledge gave them great boldness of faith to do and to act like God because they knew of a truth, it was God who lived in them.

They were men and women of great compassion.

There is a story I read once about two of William Booth's lieutenants. William Booth had founded the Salvation Army. They were called the Salvation Army because William Booth founded them and raised them as an army of soul winners. One day William Booth's lieutenants said, "We have tried everything, and we don't have revival." And William Booth said, "Go and this time try tears!"

So they went, and they came again to that great general, and they said, "Reverend Booth, we tried tears, and now we have revival."

> The Word tells us, *"That God so loved the world that He gave His only begotten son that whoever would believe in Him will not perish but have life everlasting"* (John 3:16).

God so loved. Compassion moved God. God so loved that He gave, He gave the greatest, dearest, most precious, most costly, most irreplaceable possession that He had. God so loved the whole world that He gave us, (because we were, lost in trespass and sin) His one and only Son, Jesus. Jesus Christ came to set us all free from the curse of the law, sin, sickness, poverty and death.

Can we comprehend, can we ever imagine that while we were yet sinners, the enemies of God, strangers to the covenant of promise, can we ever imagine a love so dear, so great that it would give its only son to die, in the place of it's enemy so that we may obtain everlasting life.

> The Word says in Matthew 9:36, *"But when he saw the multitudes, he was moved with compassion on them, because they fainted, and were scattered abroad, as sheep having no shepherd."*

It was love: compassion that moved Christ.

It was the joy that was set before Him that enabled Him to endure the Cross, despising the shame and He has now sat down at the right hand of the Father in Heaven. It was a love so amazing, so divine, amazing grace. Compassion that knew no earthly bounds or limitations. A love so high we can never get over it. So deep we can never get under it, so wide we can never get around it. Only by the Spirit and through the Spirit can we comprehend the height of it, the length of it, the breadth of it and the depth of it, for this love is God Himself. For the Word says that God is love, God is agape and it was this agape that moved Jesus to reach out to heal, to mend, to bind up the broken hearted and to pay the ultimate price of the sacrifice of His very life for us at Calvary. This was the compassion that these "Great Generals of the Faith", whom we admire so much, knew.

As we read and study church history, and read books like Foxes Book of Martyrs, we see the great sacrifice and price that has been paid down through the ages, so that we can have the Word of God in our hands today and our Christian freedoms in the land today. This was the compassion that these men and women possessed, that had done great exploits for the Lord. A compassion so amazing, so divine, it had been placed in their spirit by the Spirit of God, as they had hungered and thirst for righteousness.

As they had fellowshipped with God, as they had become intimate with God, what was in Him had now been birthed by His Spirit in them. It was this compassion, (God's compassion, for the lost and dying people of this world, that without the knowledge of salvation, would doom them to a dark and loveless eternal damnation) that moved them to do exploits for Jesus, for the people that do know their God (are intimate with Him) shall be strong and do exploits.

There are things that we need to recognise and develop in Christian leadership and Christian ministry. As stated above, we need to develop in the ABC's. We need to develop authority, boldness and power, Christian character and compassion. Ephesians 4:11-17 talks about authority. The power is mentioned in detail in 1 Corinthians 12 & 14, where it talks about the gifts of the Spirit. Character is the fruit of the Spirit mentioned in Galatians 5:22-25. As well as these verses, there are many other verses on these subjects. What God wants is a strong word, strong fruit and strong gifts in a solid scriptural balance.

> *"But the fruit of the Spirit is love, joy, peace, longsuffering, gentleness, goodness, faith, meekness, temperance: against such there is no law. And they that are Christ's have crucified the flesh with the affections and lusts. If we live in the Spirit, let us also walk in the Spirit"* (Galatians 5:22-25).

Two major keys to the ministry are the meditation of the Word and praying in the Spirit.

The Purpose of Tongues

God by His Holy Spirit has given you this new language to edify your spirit man, or we could say, charge up, build up and strengthen your spirit man.

> "He that speaketh in an unknown tongue edifieth himself; but he that prophesieth edifieth the church" (1 Corinthians 14:4).

> *"But ye, beloved, building up yourselves on your most holy faith, praying in the Holy Spirit"* (Jude 20).

Remember, when you are praying in the spirit, you are speaking directly to the Almighty God. At times, we do not always know what to pray, in some circumstances, with the natural mind. We might not know or understand all of the situations that are affecting us or our friends or whatever else we are going to pray for. In which case, with our natural mind, we would not know exactly how to pray God's will for the situation, but we are guaranteed in Romans 8:26 & 27 that if we pray in the spirit, that is to say, pray in tongues, we can pray the perfect will of God for any given situation.

> *"Likewise, the Spirit also helpeth our infirmities; for we know not what we should pray for as we ought; but the Spirit himself maketh intercession for us with groanings which cannot be uttered. And He that searcheth the hearts knoweth what is the mind of the Spirit, because He maketh intercession for the saints according to the will of God"* (Romans 8:26-27).

For it is the Holy Spirit who will make intercession through us in other tongues according to the perfect will of God.

What a powerful thought! What a powerful revelation! Praying in and with the Spirit is a prayer of pure faith based on the perfect will of God, because the prayer didn't originate with you. It originated with God! It originated in the realm of the spirit, the glory realm. It comes forth birthed by the Holy Spirit through your tongue, the perfect answer or outcome. You are praying the will of God for that situation or circumstance. It is just as supernatural as raising the dead because it did not originate with you, it originated with God. Can there be a better, more rewarding way to pray?

Also in Isaiah 28:11-12 in the Old Testament,

> *"For with stammering lips and another tongue will he speak to this people. To whom he said, This is the rest wherewith ye may cause the weary to rest; and this is the refreshing: yet they would not hear."*

It tells us that praying in the spirit (other tongues) is a rest and a refreshing, strengthening or renewing for the spirit. Remember, Jesus tells us in Mark 16:17 that one of the signs that follow the believer is that they will speak with new tongues.

Praying in the spirit also enlarges our comprehension or understanding of the Word of God (Ephesians 3:16 19). By praying in the spirit, we release the faith contained in the Word of God as we release God's wisdom and revelation knowledge in us. (1 Corinthians 2: 12-13).

Praying God's Perfect Will

Satan hates it when we pray in the spirit, for as we pray God's perfect will by praying as the Holy Spirit directs, we damage the kingdom of darkness.

"And these signs shall follow them that believe; In my name shall they cast out devils; they shall speak with new tongues;" (Mark 16:17).

We are living in the days of the outpouring of God's Spirit on all flesh. God promises to pour out His Spirit upon all flesh. He promises visions and dreams and supernatural gifts of the Spirit. He says, His followers, the new believers, will speak with tongues.

Praying in tongues is one of the most precious and powerful gifts of the Holy Spirit to empower your walk with God. I believe it is the key to flowing in the other gifts. If you don't have this gift, ask for it, strongly desire it and God will give it to you. Now rejoice and receive in the name of Jesus. Acts 2:16-18.

The Authority of God's Word

Some struggle with the idea of being righteous because we are all well acquainted with the Scriptures declaring man's sinfulness. The gift of righteousness is available to all who believe in Jesus Christ. Satan and the powers of darkness, regularly like to remind us of all the sins we have committed. We must now renew to the truths revealed in God's Word, concerning our righteousness.

No Fear

Righteousness is right standing with God. If I am in right standing with God, then He is not fighting against me. He is on my side. He is for me. He desires my best.

What joy will fill our hearts the day we realize *"If God be for us, who can be against us?"* (Romans 8:31). We have nothing to fear. David said, *"The Lord is my light and my salvation; whom shall I fear? The Lord is the strength of my life; of whom shall I be afraid?"* (Psalms 27:1).

God has given us the gift of righteousness because of His love for us.

> *"There is no fear in love; but perfect love casteth out fear: because fear hath torment. He that feareth is not made perfect in love"* (1 John 4:18).

A loving father does not want his children to be so fearful of him that they are afraid to talk to him. He desires their respect, reverence, and obedience, but he wants them to feel comfortable coming to him. God invites us to *"come boldly unto the throne of grace that we may obtain mercy and find grace to help in time of need"* (Hebrews 4:16). *"For God hath not given us the spirit of fear; but of power, and of love, and of a sound mind"* (2 Timothy 1:7). No Inferiority.

Reign in Life

Occasionally when someone is asked how they are doing, we hear them respond with these words: "Under the circumstances, I think I'll make it." As Christians, thank God, we do not have to be 'under the circumstances', in fact, after we receive the abundance of God's grace and His gift of righteousness, we are to reign in this life by Jesus Christ.

Because I have a right standing with God, I do not have to feel inferior to the powers of Satan. I am an heir of God and a joint-heir with Christ (Romans 8:17). As we receive the righteousness of God, we become partakers of the divine nature of God (2 Peter 1:4). His strength has become our strength. His ability is our ability. His life is our life.

> *"I am crucified with Christ: Nevertheless I live; yet not I, but CHRIST LIVETH IN ME: and the life which I now live in the flesh I LIVE BY THE FAITH OF THE SON OF GOD, who loved me and gave himself for me"* (Galatians 2:20).

Continual Cleansing from Unrighteousness

As Christians, we may miss the mark and sin. Sin is unrighteousness. It is not pleasing to God. It must be dealt with. The best time to do this is immediately, if not sooner. Do not wait to repent, just repent!

> The promise of God is, *"If we confess our sins, He is faithful and just to* **FORGIVE US OUR SINS***, and to* **CLEANSE US FROM ALL UNRIGHTEOUSNESS"** *(1 John 1:9). "...the* **BLOOD** *of Jesus Christ His Son* **CLEANSETH** *us from all sin"* (1 John 1:7).

Our Prayers are Effective

With a right standing with God, we can come boldly into His presence with our praises and petitions (Hebrews 4:16).

One of the most important things we must do as we enter into God's presence is to be sure our hearts are cleansed from all sin. This comes by faith in the cleansing power of the blood of Christ. After we know we are cleansed, we can have confidence in our prayers.

> *"Beloved, if our heart condemn us not, then have we confidence towards God"* (1 John 3:21).

God delights in hearing the prayers of His righteous children. *"For the eyes of the Lord are over the righteous, and His ears are open unto their prayers: but the face of the Lord is against them that do evil"* (1 Peter 3:12). Evidently, if we are not righteous or if we are not seeking God's righteousness, our prayers will not be very effective.

Thank God, *"The effectual fervent prayer of a righteous man availeth much"* (James 5:16). God will hear and answer our prayers if we maintain our right standing (righteousness in Christ) by faith.

God's Word Must be Confessed

What a person says with his mouth can either release or negate (cancel out) what he believes in his heart. Not only does God desire His children to believe His Word, but also to speak and obey His Word. Jesus said "out of the abundance of the heart the mouth speaketh" (Matthew 12:34). Our mouths actually reveal what is in our hearts. Jesus explained the connection between the mouth and heart in this way:

> "A good man out of the good treasure of the heart bringeth forth good things: and an evil man out of the evil treasure bringeth forth evil things. But I say unto you, that every idle word that men shall speak, they shall give account thereof in the day of judgment. For by thy words thou shalt be justified, and by thy words thou shalt be condemned" (Matthew 12:35-37).

It does not take long to realize that Jesus believes that what we say is important. Our words will either justify or condemn us. There will be an account given of the words spoken by our mouth. If they are not according to the truth of God's Word, they will be idle, meaningless, and often times, very destructive.

Death and Life in the Tongue

> "Death and life are in the power of the tongue: and they that love it shall eat the fruit thereof." (Proverbs 18:21 in the Old Testament).

This is practically the same thing Jesus said. The tongue can either work for us or against us. It is never a neutral force because it is usually speaking words of life or words of death. The words a man speaks create the blessings or curses that come his way in life. It is definitely God's desire to bless His children. But we must believe, speak, and obey God's Word BEFORE we can receive God's blessings.

> "Thou art snared with the words of thy mouth, thou art taken with the words of thy mouth" (Proverbs 6:2).

The words we speak determine the life we enjoy. The reason is that our mouth is a revealer of the beliefs in our heart. If heart and mouth both get in accord with God's Word, then the blessings of God's Word begin to be tapped.

"A man's belly shall be satisfied with the fruit of his mouth; and with the increase of his lips shall he be filled" (Proverbs 18:20).

Salvation, blessing, prosperity, victory, and joy are all promised in God's Word. The man who receives them is the one who believes the promise and begins to confess it with his mouth.

Believe and Confess

*"But what saith it? The Word is nigh thee, even in thy **MOUTH**, and in thy **HEART:** that is the **WORD OF FAITH**, which we preach; that if thou shalt **CONFESS WITH THY MOUTH** the Lord Jesus, and shalt **BELIEVE IN THINE HEART** that God hath raised him from the dead, thou shalt be saved. For with the **HEART** man **BELIEVETH** unto righteousness; and with the **MOUTH CONFESSION** is made unto salvation"* (Romans 10:8-10).

Paul preached the word of faith to the people in Rome. He told them that this Word is in two places: in their heart to believe, and in their mouth to confess. This Scripture tells us that confession is part of salvation, just as believing is part of salvation.

Whenever we hear the good news of God's Word, it is up to us to believe and confess it personally. Thus we begin the important process of both hearing and doing the Word. Jesus equated this to a man building his house upon the rock. (Matthew 7:24).

Keep the Word in Your Mouth

God has given us a formula for success as we go about our daily routine of living. It is a message that He spoke first to Joshua concerning his success as a leader of Israel.

> *"This book of the law shall not depart out of thy mouth; but thou shalt meditate therein day and night, that thou mayest observe to do according to all that is written therein: for then thou shalt make thy way prosperous, and then thou shalt have good success"* (Joshua 1:8 in the Old Testament).

The formula for success that God gave to Joshua was:
1. Keep the Word (book of the Law) in your mouth.
2. Meditate day and night in that Word.
3. Do what the Word says.

Notice that God said Joshua would make his own way prosperous by doing these things. He would not only have success, but it would be *"good success"*.

It is no wonder that David prayed to God,
> *"Let the words of my mouth, and the meditation of my heart be acceptable in Thy sight, O Lord, my*

Strength, and my Redeemer" (Psalm 19:14 Old Testament).

David knew that his own success greatly depended upon his meditation and confession. He had experienced a tremendous victory as a teenager because of meditating God's Word and boldly speaking it forth in the face of Goliath (1 Samuel 17:45-50 Old Testament). Remember, he spoke words of faith **BEFORE** the giant fell. Anyone can shout after the victory is won, but it takes faith to shout **BEFORE** the walls fall (Joshua 6:16).

The important thing to remember in faith confession is that God's Word must be the foundation. We must know the truth and be convinced concerning God's will (2 Timothy 2:15). Then God will back our confession, because he is faithful to keep His Word (Numbers 23:19).

No Corrupt Communication

Begin to speak forth God's Word, believing He will bring it to pass. At the same time, stop speaking negative words that are contrary to the Word of God. In the beginning, this may seem a little strange, but it will become a tremendous blessing. Make a decision to say as David says, "Set a watch O Lord, before my mouth; keep the door of my lips" (Psalm 141:3 Old Testament).

Refrain from speaking anything evil, negative, critical, or idle. If I must say something, then I think first and speak about, *"whatsoever things are true, whatsoever things are honest, whatsoever things are just, whatsoever things are pure, whatsoever things are lovely, whatsoever things are of good report"* (Philippians 4:8).

Generally, a person cannot improve a situation by speaking negatively about it. Nor can he help someone by criticising them without love. But if a person speaks God's Word over the situation or person, he has released his faith and brought the power of the Lord on the scene.

> *"Let no corrupt communication proceed out of your mouth, but that which is good to the use of edifying, that it may minister grace unto the hearers"* (Ephesians 4:29).

Every time we speak, we hear ourselves and God hears us. By speaking the Words of life, we can minister to ourselves and to God, not to mention what it will do in the lives of others that hear our conversation.

Overcoming by the Word of our Testimony

Those that overcome Satan will be required to use the power of the spoken Word. It is the sword of the spirit in the Christian's armour (Ephesians 6:17). Jesus spoke the Word aloud directly to Satan in the wilderness (Matthew 4:1-11), thus giving a battle-plan to the Christian on how to defeat the devil. We can resist the devil with the Word and he will flee (James 4:7).

> *"And they overcame him by the blood of the lamb, and by the word of their testimony; and they loved not their lives unto the death"* (Revelation 12:11).

The blood of Jesus cleanses us from all sin and frees us from all condemnation from Satan (1 John 1:7, Romans 8:1). The word of our testimony is the sword that puts Satan to flight. It is the Word of God coming from our lips that produces an overcoming spirit in us.

Speak to the Mountain

Jesus said, "Have faith in God. For verily I say unto you, that whosoever shall say unto this mountain, Be thou removed, and be thou cast into the sea; and shall not doubt in his heart, but shall believe that those things which he saith shall come to pass; he shall have whatsoever he saith" (Mark 11:22-23).

Jesus said the person who believes in his heart what he says with his mouth, would have what he says. It is true we have the things we believe and speak. For instance, the person who believes he is going to get angry over a situation and then says, "I'm going to get mad," usually will get mad. This just seems to work in every area of life. The reason is because it is a spiritual law. It works whether we believe it or not. It is the same as the physical law of gravity - it works regardless of our attitude towards it.

If I believe God's Word is true for me, then I can begin to claim it's promises by confessing them in my life. Faith requires me to speak them before I feel or see them.

If there is a mountain of a problem in my life, family, body, or finances, I must speak directly to the problem. As I speak,

I must believe that what I say will come to pass. God says that what I say will become a visible reality in the natural world if I steadfastly hold to my confession of faith.

There is power in our mouth. The belief in our heart is released by faith out of our mouth. By believing, confessing, and acting on God's Word, we can receive salvation, healing, the Holy Spirit, righteousness, and a victorious abundant life. All of these are promised to the Christian and available by faith.

Understanding the Authority of God's Word

Understanding the authority of God's Word, as stated, is also a major key. We know that God has established authority. Authority is not something that you can have in only one part of your life. You can't submit in authority to God and not submit to authority in other ways.

This is the mistake Christian men and women make many times. They think I can submit to the authority of God, and rebel at the authority that God has instituted in their life in other ways. That adds up to rebellion and perversion. The principle of authority must be instilled in you and in me in order for us to submit to God as the authority, and anyone else He has placed in authority. The reason many Christians, today, can't mature in Jesus is that they want to be submitted to the authority of the Word (to a greater or lesser extent as long as it doesn't interfere with something else they believe), but not to the authority God has established. Authority is a complete principle. The centurion soldier recognised that Jesus had authority because He was under, submitted to and yielded to that authority. You can't just have authority in part of your life, you must come to a place where you recognise there is authority, there is power, there is character and allow all of these things to operate in your life.

You will never permit God to do the work inside of you unless you submit to it, yield to the authority of the Holy Spirit and the Word in you.

One day I said to God, "Lord, if you can't have authority unless you are under authority, then how come you have authority?

Lord what authority are you under, for You have all authority?" He said to me, "Shaun, I am under and submitted to the authority of my Word. I have exalted my Word higher than My Name."

Wow! That blew my mind. That was powerful. Then we see Jesus, who is the Word, submit Himself to the Father. So then, the Godhead is submitted to the authority of God, and that authority is the Word. The Godhead is all completely submitted to the Word. The Word of God is final authority in all of creation.

> *"I will worship toward your holy temple, and praise your name for your lovingkindness and for your truth: for you have magnified your word above all your name"* (Psalm 138:2).

What to Expect When You Fast

1. Fasting makes the will of God known.
2. Fasting will launch your ministry.
3. Fasting will bring forth your healing ministry.
4. Fasting will cause one to be well tuned to the Spirit.
5. Fasting will cause you to be recognised in the spirit realm.
6. Fasting will cause one to bring the flesh under submission.
7. Fasting brings holiness into our lives.
8. Fasting causes an overflow of the Spirit.
9. Fasting causes us to help others.
10. Fasting causes us to wait on God.
11. Fasting causes us to overcome the devourer.
12. Fasting causes us to loose the captives, oppressed and those bound.
13. Fasting restores what has been destroyed.
14. Fasting restores a conquering spirit.
15. Fasting causes us to gain recognition with God.
16. Fasting causes us to gain recognition with man.
17. Fasting causes revival to come.
18. Fasting sets the captives free.
19. Fasting restores what has been stolen.
20. Fasting causes loved ones to be loosened.
21. Fasting causes us to hear the voice of God.
22. Fasting causes prophecy to be fulfilled.
23. Fasting causes us to take charge in the spirit realm.
24. Fasting causes us to reign supreme over the enemy.
25. Fasting speeds up results that, otherwise take years to happen.
26. Fasting causes us to destroy the works of Satan.
27. Fasting causes us to gain influence with God.
28. Fasting brings about an awareness of God's presence.
29. Fasting is a way of seeking God.

30. Fasting is a way of touching God.
31. Fasting is a way of ministering to God.

And that is why I call it 'The Fast Way to Power'! Remember Paul said, *"that I might know Him and the power of His resurrection"* (Philippians 3:10a). Jesus said *"You shall receive power after the Holy Spirit has come upon you"* (Acts 1:8). By fasting we yield ourselves to God, aligning ourselves with His will and allowing the power and anointing of the Holy Spirit to flow through us.

God wants to do something in you so He can do something through you.

Chapter Three

THE CURE FOR UNBELIEF

The disciples asked the Lord why they could not heal a lunatic boy. Jesus said, "Because of your unbelief... Howbeit this kind, goeth not out but by prayer and fasting" (Matthew 17:14-21). Faith needs prayer for its development and full growth, and prayer needs fasting for the same reason. Fasting has done wonders when used in combination with prayer and faith. This is a biblical doctrine. To fast means to abstain from food – that which caused the fall of man. Fasting humbles the soul before God (Psalm 35:13); chastens, corrects the soul (Psalm 69:10); and crucifies the appetites and denies them, so as to give entire time to prayer (2 Samuel 12:16-23; Matthew 4:1-11). It manifests earnestness before God, to the exclusion of all else (1 Corinthians 7:5); shows obedience; gives the digestive system a rest (Matthew 6:16-18; 9:15; Luke 5:33); demonstrates the mastery of man over appetites; aids in temptation; helps to attain power over demons; develops faith; crucifies unbelief; and aids in prayer (Matthew 4:1-11; 17:14-21).

"Then was Jesus led up of the Spirit into the wilderness to be tempted of the devil. And when he had fasted forty days and forty nights, he was afterward an hungred. And when the tempter came to him, he said, If thou be the Son of God, command that these stones be made bread. But he answered and said, It is written, Man shall not live by bread alone, but by every word that proceedeth out of the mouth of God. Then the devil taketh him up into the holy city, and setteth him on a pinnacle of the temple, and saith unto him, If thou be the Son of God, cast thyself down: for it is written, He shall give his angels charge concerning thee: and in their hands they shall bear thee up, lest at any time thou dash thy foot against a stone. Jesus said unto him, It is written again, Thou shalt not tempt the Lord thy God. Again, the devil taketh him up into an exceeding high mountain, and sheweth him all the kingdoms of the world, and the glory of them; And saith unto him, All these things will I give thee, if thou wilt fall down and worship me. Then saith Jesus unto him, Get thee hence, Satan: for it is written, Thou shalt worship the Lord thy God, and him only shalt thou serve. Then the devil leaveth him, and, behold, angels came and ministered unto him" (Matthew 4:1-11).

"And when they were come to the multitude, there came to him a certain man, kneeling down to him, *and saying, Lord, have mercy on my son: for he is lunatick, and sore vexed: for ofttimes he falls into the fire, and oft into the water. And I brought him to thy disciples, and they could not cure him. Then Jesus answered and said, O faithless and perverse generation, how long shall I be with you? how long shall I suffer you? bring him hither to me. And Jesus rebuked the devil; and he departed out of him: and the child was cured from that very hour. Then came the disciples to Jesus apart, and said, Why could not we cast him out? And Jesus said unto them, Because of your unbelief: for verily I say unto you, If ye have faith as a grain of mustard seed, ye shall say unto this mountain, Remove hence to yonder place; and it shall remove; and nothing shall be impossible unto you. Howbeit this kind goes not out but by prayer and fasting"* (Matthew 17:14-21).

All believers are supposed to fast, but no regulations or set rules are given as to how long or how often. That is determined by individual desire and needs (Matthew 9:14-15; 1 Corinthians 7:5; Acts 13:1-5). Men should fast when under chastening or correction (2 Samuel 12:16-23); under judgment (1 Kings 21:27); in need (Ezra 8:21); in danger (Esther 4); when worried (Daniel 6:18); in trouble (Acts 27:9, 33) in spiritual conflict (Matthew 4:1-11); and when desperate in prayer (Acts 9).

35 Bible Fasts

WHO FASTED?	LENGTH	REFERENCE
1. Ahab	?	1 Kings 21:27-29
2. Judah	?	2 Chronicles 20:1-25
3. Judah	?	Ezra 8:21-23
4. Ezra	?	Ezra 10:6-17
5. Nineveh	?	Jonah 3
6. Nehemiah	?	Nehemiah 1:4-2:10
7. Jews	?	Esther 4:1-3, 9:1-3
8. David	?	Psalm 35:13, 69:10, 109:24
9. John's disciples	?	Matthew 9:14-15
10. Anna	?	Luke 2:37
11. Church at Antioch	?	Acts 13:1-5
12. Paul	?	Acts 27:9-11
13. Cornelius	?	Acts 10
14. Many churches	?	Acts 14:23
15. Paul	?	2 Corinthians 6:5; 11:27
16. David	1 Day	2 Samuel 3:35
17. Judah	1 Day	Nehemiah 9:1-4
18. Judah	1 Day	Jeremiah 36:6
19. Daniel	1 Day	Daniel 9:3 - 27
20. Pharisee	1 Day	Luke 18:9-14
21. Israel	1 Day	Judges 20:26-35
22. Israel	1 Day	1 Samuel 7:6-14
23. King David	1 Day	2 Samuel 1:12
24. Darius	1 Night	Daniel 6:18-24
25. Esther, Mordecai	3 days	Esther 4:13-16, 5:1-9:3
26. Many people	3 days	Matthew 15:32-39
27. Paul	3 days	Acts 9:9 - 17
28. David	7 days	2 Samuel 12:16-23

29. Israel	7 days	1 Samuel 31:13
30. Paul & 276 men	14 days	Acts 27:33-34
31. Daniel	21 days	Daniel 10:3-13
32. Moses	40 days	Deu9:9,18,25-29; 10:10
33. Joshua	40 days	Exodus 24:13-18; 32:15-17
34. Elijah	40 days	1 Kings 19:7-18
35. Jesus	40 days	Matthew 4:1-11

Since fasting and prayer are so prominent in the Bible, modern Christians should do more of this until they receive power with God over all the powers of the devil. Many things about fasting and its benefits are not known to modern men, but those through the ages who have been men of great prayer have also fasted much.

Chapter Four

THE IMPORTANCE OF FASTING

Jesus went up the mountain many times to pray.

It was after prayer that He cast the demons out of the child.

When His disciples asked Him why they could not cast the demon out... Jesus replied, *"This kind can come forth by nothing but by prayer and fasting."* Matthew 17:21.

Jesus did not have to run quickly to the mountain to pray and fast; He had already prayed and fasted and was ready for action.

Prayer and fasting were part of His daily life. They met the need.

Fasting is important because God has ordained it in His Word.

Fasting is an important part of self-denial, or denial of the flesh.

One of the strongest desires of the flesh is food... it is during a fast that one denies himself food.

Eating in itself is not sinful, but to give it undue importance, putting it before God and His blessings, makes it a sin.

Paul warned his church at Philippi of some whom they might be tempted to follow, *"For many walk, of whom I have told you often, and now tell you even weeping, that they are the enemies of the cross of Christ: Whose end is destruction, whose god is their belly, and whose glory is in their shame, who mind earthly things."* Philippians 3:18-19.

It was for food that the first temptation occurred in the Garden of Eden (Genesis 3:1-6).

It was for food that Esau despised and sold his birthright (Genesis 25:32).

It was for food that Satan directed the first temptation to Jesus when He was in the wilderness (Matthew 4:3).

Paul declared that he was in fastings often (2 Corinthians 11:27).

> *"In weariness and painfulness, in watchings often, in hunger and thirst, in fastings often, in cold and nakedness"* (2 Corinthians 11:27).

Many are hindered from receiving the miracle-working power of God in their lives, because they would rather eat and not miss a good meal than receive a blessing from God.

If you want what God has, you have to be willing to do a little self denying.

Discipline; when your goals are more important to you than your pleasure, leisure.

Fasting itself cannot accomplish miracles unless you do it right.

> The Israelites in Isaiah's day cried out, *"Wherefore have we fasted, and Thou seest not?* God's reply through His prophet was, *"Behold, in the day of your fast ye find pleasure, and exact all your finding. Behold ye fast for strife and debate, and to smite with the fist of wickedness. Ye shall not fast as ye do this day, to make your voice to be heard on high"* (Isaiah 58:3-4).

If our fasting is to help any by making our voice to be heard on High, it must be done unselfishly, if it is to be done effectively.

It must also include an enlarged vision of our responsibility to be our brother's keeper.

God said, *"Is not this the fast that I have chosen?"* Isaiah 58:5-9.

1. To loose the bonds of wickedness.
2. To undo the heavy burdens.
3. To let the oppressed go free.
4. To break every yoke.

"Is it not to deal thy bread to the hungry, and that thou bring the poor that are cast out to thy house? When thou seest the naked that thou cover him; and that thou hide not thyself from thine own flesh? Then shall thy light break forth as the morning and thine health shall spring forth speedily: and thy righteousness shall go before thee; the glory of the Lord shall be thy rearward. Then shalt thou call, and the Lord shall answer; thou take away from the midst of thee the yoke, and putting forth of the finger, and speaking vanity" (Isaiah 58:5-9).

You must have the right motive when you fast. Some have the attitude, *"If I fast, then I can get God to do what I want Him to do."* Then they wonder why nothing happened when they fasted.

Fasting does not obligate God to do what you want Him to do. Fasting is to humble our heart before God and to seek His face for a revelation of His will to be accomplished.

You see, fasting is one of God's laws that will make this happen. When we fast we will find that as Isaiah said, "the bonds will be loosened".

This is God speaking. This is God saying to the church, to the believer, *"Is not this the fast that I have chosen?"* This is God showing us, right here, in His Word, that He has chosen a way that we can take care of the bonds, that we can take care of the sick, that we can take care of the burdens, that we can take care of everything that makes people oppressed and brings them into a state where people are controlled and under the power of the devil.

God has said, *"I will tell you how you can liberate them. I have chosen a kind of fast that will get the job done."*

Verse 7 says, *"I have chosen this fast... to deal thy bread to the hungry".*

God is saying to us, *"I want you to be able to deal bread to the hungry".* This is spiritual. This is referring to people who have a spiritual need: people who are naked spiritually, those who have been cast out of their spiritual house and don't know God and are not walking with God, and those whom the devil is taking around in a circle.

God said, *"Is not this the fast that I have chosen that you might deal bread to the hungry, that you might take the people who are cast out, that are under oppression to bring them to a place where they get to know Me and get to know My Word and don't have to hide from their own flesh."*

Some of God's people are running in circles, trying to stay saved. They say, "Oh, if I can just stay saved." And most of their prayers are, "Lord, I committed another sin, forgive me."

God doesn't want us to run in a circle. He doesn't want us to live a kind of life where all we have is an up-down yo-yo experience. God wants us to move into His realm and be dynamite in His hands.

How many people would like their health to spring forth speedily? You may have been trying for years to get a little bit of sickness or pain out of your body. Would you like for your health to spring forth speedily? God has chosen a fast to do it. It's in the Word.

Now read Isaiah 58:12. A waste place is a place that has become desolate. It is a place that has been broken down. It has no foundation. You have some people in your family that the devil has caused to become like a waste place. You know, no doubt, someone who has had their foundation pulled out from under them by Satan. They are people who don't have an experience with God. So the Bible tells us, *"And they shall be of thee that shall build the old waste places. Thou shall raise up the foundations, and many generations, and thou shall be called the repairer of the breach and the restorer of the paths to dwell in."* Isaiah 58:12.

In other words, God is saying that you are going to do a repair job on your loved ones and on your family. This will come through salvation, through deliverance and through healing. Everything they need you are going to restore and repair so they can be what God has called them to be. They will be what God originally intended them to be.

God wants to put us in the place so that every demon that comes against mankind will have to yield to us. He wants us to be a repairer of people. But you cannot repair lives, you cannot restore the lives, and you cannot repair or build up the foundation until first of all, you come into that place with God that comes only through prayer and fasting.

What God is going to do for us can only be done as you and I are dedicated. And it isn't how long you fast. It is how much dedication we put into what we are doing.

Several things should happen:
1. You come into a place of humility before God.
2. You will become more consecrated.
3. You will come into a place of holiness.
4. You will be willing to change.
5. Your life will be changed and shaken.

Then you will find your spiritual bonds are loosened and you will be established in the spiritual world. And most of all your spirit man will begin to respond to you instead of you responding to the flesh.

Do you know that most of our lives are spent doing what our flesh tells us to do? Most of our lives are spent with us bowing down to the desires of our flesh.

You may say, "Oh, no that is not true." Alright, then let me put a nice piece of apple pie that is sizzling with steam in front of you, with cream and ice-cream. Then we will see how long you can contain yourself.

But, when we go on the fast that He has chosen, to accomplish the four things listed on page 59, we will see our "light break forth as the morning", and our "health shall spring forth speedily," and our "righteousness shall go before us", and the greatest of all, "the glory of the Lord shall be our rear guard." Then we will see the anointing break the yoke and the power of God go into operation.

It is not enough to do the right thing. Our hearts and motives must be right when we do the right thing. Then God will honour it and bless it.

When fasting is done God's way, then His promises will come to pass.

Not every fast is acceptable to God (Matthew 6:16-18).

Those who boasted about fasting were branded by Jesus as hypocrites.

He recommended that fasting be done in private, secretly between God and the individual.

When fasting is done this way, God will hear from heaven and reward you openly by answering your prayers.

True fasting gives God first place over all other demands of life.

The husband and wife should agree on a fast and rule out personal gratification during that period, so that God may be put first.

God does not condemn marriage: He instituted, ordained and blessed it as the relationship between husband and wife. But like the desire for food, sex is also a strong desire of the flesh. This desire, too, should be set aside for a time while seeking God and the profit that comes from God.

"The wife hath not power of her own body, but the husband: and likewise also the husband hath not

power of his own body, but the wife. Defraud ye not one another, except it be with consent for a time, that ye may give yourselves to fasting and prayer; and come together again, that Satan tempt you not for your incontinency" (1 Corinthians 7:4-5).

Self-denial will many times take you out of the company which you find most enjoyable, even though the company you keep is good.

Power with God comes through fellowship with God. 1 John 1:3.

"That which we have seen and heard declare we unto you, that ye also may have fellowship with us: and truly our fellowship is with the Father, and with his Son Jesus Christ" (1 John 1:3).

Those who have power with God are:

1. Setting the captives free.
2. Bringing deliverance to many.
3. Winning souls.

They are those who spend time alone with God before they spend time with people!

People in the Bible Who Have Fasted

1.　　NEHEMIAH fasted and prayed certain days for himself and for Israel. Nehemiah 1:4.

2. KING DAVID adorned himself in sackcloth to fast and pray. Psalms 35:13.

3. EZRA fasted and mourned because of the peoples' transgression. Ezra 10:6.

4. NINEVEH fasted to prevent God destroying them and their city. Jonah 3:5-10.

5. ANNA the eighty-four year old prophetess, served God with fasting and prayer night and day. Luke 2:37.

6. THE CHURCH AT ANTIOCH fasted and prayed, then laid hands on Barnabas and Saul for the work to which they were called. Acts 13:1-3.

7. PAUL fasted and prayed during the storm when sailing became dangerous and the crew fearful. Acts 27:9-11.

8. JEREMIAH fasted for one day. Jeremiah 36:6.

9. DARIUS fasted for one night while Daniel was in the lions' den. Daniel 6:18.

10. ESTHER fasted for three days when Israel was in danger. Esther 4:16.

11. DAVID fasted for seven days. 2 Samuel 12:16-20.

12. PAUL fasted for fourteen days. Acts 27:33-35.

13. DANIEL fasted for twenty-one days. Daniel 10:3.

14. JOSHUA fasted for forty days. Exodus 24:12-18.

15. MOSES fasted for forty days. Exodus 24:12-18 & Deuteronomy 9:9.

16. ELIJAH fasted for forty days. 1 Kings 19:8.

17. JESUS fasted for forty days. Matthew 4:2.

CHAPTER FIVE

RESULTS OF FASTING

Fasting Brings Deliverance

Isaiah 58:6 *"Is not this the fast that I have chosen to loose the bands of wickedness, to undo the heavy burdens and to let the oppressed go free, and that ye break every yoke?"*

Fasting Brings Revelation

Daniel 9:3, 21-22 *"And I set my face unto the Lord God, to seek by prayer and supplications, with fasting, and sackcloth, and ashes: Yea, while I was speaking in prayer, even the man Gabriel, who I had seen in the vision at the beginning, being caused to fly swiftly, touched me about the time of the evening oblation. And he informed me, and talked with me, and said, O Daniel, I am now come forth to give thee skill and understanding."*

1. Revelation concerning God's will.

2. Revelation concerning God's word.

3. Revelation concerning divine wisdom.

4. Revelation concerning how to handle a crisis.

Personally, I have always received great revelations from the Lord during and after my times of prayer and fasting.

Fasting Brings Visions

> *"'And now I exhort you to be of good cheer: for there shall be no loss of any man's life among you, but of the ship. For there stood by me this night the angel of God, whose I am, and whom I serve, saying, 'Fear not, Paul' Thou must be brought before Caesar: and lo, God hath given thee all them that sail with thee.' Wherefore, sirs, be of good cheer: for I believe God, that it shall be even as it was told me"* (Acts 27:22-25).
>
> *Wherefore I pray you to take some meat; for there shall not be a hair fall from the head of any of you. And when he had thus spoken, he took bread; and gave thanks to God in the presence of them all; and when he had broken it, he began to eat. Then were they all of good cheer, and they also took some meat"* (Acts 27:34-36).

For three days these men had battled a storm that threatened to sink the ship and drown all aboard. The ship was "exceedingly tossed" and all hope of being saved was gone. There was no time to eat or sleep for the severity of the storm. Then the angel of the Lord came and brought assurance and peace. Then they broke bread and ate meat.

Fasting Brings Victory

Victory over iniquity, evil thoughts, habits, and help to gain a pure heart. 2 Timothy 2:21-22 *"If a man therefore purge himself from these, he shall be a vessel unto honour, sanctified, and fit for the master's use, and prepared unto every good work. Flee also youthful lusts: but follow righteousness, faith, love (charity), peace, with them that call on the Lord out of a pure heart."*

We are warned to flee youthful lusts. This does not only mean youthful as a number of years that you have lived, but in comparing "youthful and mature" in our Christian walk. Until you begin to grow spiritually, the lusts of the flesh will continually try to control you and your life.

You must continue to feed on the Word of God and pray. By doing this, you will purge yourself from the dictates of the flesh and become a vessel of honour, one that is sanctified and ready for the Master's use. You will have a desire to follow after righteousness and call on the Lord out of a pure heart.

Spiritual Warfare

We are in a battle for freedom. A full on war with the powers of darkness, but we are not alone, the Lord declares *"THE BATTLE IS MINE THE VICTORY IS YOURS."* This is God's war. He has taken responsibility for the battle and has declared the outcome! Christians are VICTORIOUS!

Now then God has given us PRECISE instructions in His Word to ensure this favourable outcome. To guarantee this VICTORY! To pray always and to fast often is a mighty part of these instructions. I am convinced, that revival is possible anywhere people will dedicate themselves to these tasks. It is historically true that prayer has been the key to every revival in the history of Christianity.

You find the followers of Christ (the Disciples, disciplined followers) in prayer before the Church was birthed in the book of Acts 2.

> *"And they worshipped him, and returned to Jerusalem with great joy: And were continually in the temple, praising and blessing God. Amen"* (Luke 24:52 & 53). SO BE IT!

Acts 1:14 (a) *"These all continued with one accord in prayer and supplication ..."* Before the great outpouring of Pentecost came.

I believe the power of fasting combined with prayer is the spiritual atomic bomb that our Lord has given us, to destroy the strongholds of evil and usher in a great revival and spiritual harvest around the world!

This revival and spiritual harvest will be the greatest harvest in the history of the Church, the greatest move of God this earth has ever seen. But before God comes in revival power, the Holy Spirit will call millions of God's people to repent, fast and pray in the Spirit of 2 Chronicles 7:14.

> *"If my people, which are called by my name, shall humble themselves, and pray, and seek my face, and turn from their wicked ways; then will I hear from heaven, and will forgive their sin, and will heal their land"* (2 Chronicles 7:14).

Today peoples' hearts are dry! It is like we are in a dry place where no water is. The good news is this, the drier the wood, the quicker it sets ablaze when someone throws a match in. Prayer and Fasting will be that match! Amen!

The task for world evangelism remains the same. It is unchanged. God has not changed in the slightest degree and He has promised to help us! **God will do for us what He did for the Apostles if we do for God what the Apostles did.**

God has not changed in His dealings with us. We know God by the way He deals with us. If it ever changed then it would be meaningless to say God never changes. If God dealt with Paul differently from the way He deals with us then how can He be a faithful God? But God is faithful. The God we trust is the one we know through the revelation of Scripture. He never does anything out of character. God is faithful to what He is and He is His Word! That is why we can sing great is thy faithfulness oh God!

God's will has not changed either. His will is sovereign but it is not unknown. It is revealed to us in His WORD.

If we are to "observe" the original apostolic ministry , the book of Acts is where we will see the most. Here we see the CHURCH as it was meant to be! If you will spend several months in close study of this book you will be profoundly stirred and to be honest, you will also be disturbed.

Stirred, because a body of ordinary men and women, joined in an unconquerable fellowship, in unity never before seen on this earth.

Disturbed, because this is the Church, how it was meant to be.

These are the days before the Church became fat and short of breath through prosperity, or muscle bound over organisation. These men did not make "Acts of Faith" they believed and did "Acts of Faith!" They did not say their prayers, they really prayed. They did not hold conferences on psychosomatic medicine, they simply healed the sick!

By modern standards the disciples may have been naïve, but because of their simplicity, their readiness to simply believe, to obey, to give, to suffer and if necessary to die, the Spirit of God found He could work in them and through them, so they turned the world upside down!

Everyone who has ever been used of God went through a process called "the period of preparation". They had battles, persecutions and oppositions, but the end result was a great ministry and a great VICTORY!

Great men and women such as Elijah, Elisha, Moses, Jesus, Esther and Anna the prophetess, not only prayed but also fasted during the period of preparation.

Fasting and prayer will give God's direction for our lives and work, if it is done as unto the Lord (Acts 13:2).

Jesus has said His disciples will fast often. Sometimes the very thought of fasting causes anxiety, fear and a negative reaction - I can't do that! Why? This is because the number one desire of the flesh is for food. From the time we are born, even for comfort, a mother will put a bottle in a baby's mouth every time it cries. <u>We grow up with the concept that food answers all things.</u> I know myself, lots of times when the pressure is on you are drawn to the fridge. Most of us have been guilty, at some time of comfort eating.

People, we design our whole days around food. After breakfast we will catch up. Before lunch, I'm doing such and such. Let's meet for coffee. I'll ring you after dinner.

> Jesus said to His disciples *"If any man will come after me, let him deny himself and take up his cross, and follow me"* (In Matthew 16:24).

Fasting is praying with the body.

Look at the result in Matthew 16:24-28, *"Then said Jesus unto his disciples, If any man will come after me, let him deny himself, and take up his cross, and follow me. For whosoever will save his life shall lose it: and whosoever will lose his life for my sake shall find it. For what is a man profited, if he shall gain the whole world, and lose his own soul? or what shall a man give in exchange for his soul? For the Son of man shall come in the glory of his Father with his angels; and then he shall reward every man according to his works. Verily I say unto you, there be some standing here, which shall not taste of death, till they see the Son of man coming in his kingdom."*

In the Strong's Concordance we find the meaning of the word 'fast': a primitive root, to cover over (the mouth) ie to fast.

- We humble ourself by fasting.
- We correct ourself by fasting.
- We serve God by fasting.

We are to seek the Lord, for in Him are hidden all things that are precious. "In Whom are hid all treasures of wisdom and knowledge" Colossians 2:3.

Fasting Examples

"But as for me, when they were sick, my clothing was sackcloth: I humbled my soul with fasting; and

my prayer returned into mine own bosom. I behaved myself as though he had been my friend or brother: I bowed down heavily, as one that mourneth for his mother" (Psalm 35:13-14).

A fast to bring healing and deliverance to the people of the earth.

"And in every province, whithersoever the king's commandment and his decree came, there was great mourning among the Jews, and fasting, and weeping, and wailing; and many lay in sackcloth and ashes" (Esther 4:3).

"Now in the twenty and fourth day of this month the children of Israel were assembled with fasting, and with sackclothes, and earth upon them" (Nehemiah 9:1).

"And he was there with the LORD forty days and forty nights; he did neither eat bread, nor drink water. And he wrote upon the tables the words of the covenant, the ten commandments. And it came to pass, when Moses came down from mount Sinai with the two tables of testimony in Moses' hand, when he came down from the mount, that Moses wist not that the skin of his face shone while he talked with him. And when Aaron and all the children of Israel saw Moses, behold, the skin of his face shone;

and they were afraid to come nigh him. And Moses called unto them; and Aaron and all the rulers of the congregation returned unto him: and Moses talked with them. And afterward all the children of Israel came nigh: and he gave them in commandment all that the LORD had spoken with him in mount Sinai. And till Moses had done speaking with them, he put a vail on his face. But when Moses went in before the LORD to speak with him, he took the vail off, until he came out. And he came out, and spake unto the children of Israel that which he was commanded. And the children of Israel saw the face of Moses, that the skin of Moses' face shone: and Moses put the vail upon his face again, until he went in to speak with him" (Exodus 34:28-35).

Moses fasted 40 days and 40 nights while on Horeb the MOUNT OF GOD. But this was a supernatural fast as he ate not food. Neither did he drink water. Moses was supernaturally sustained by the presence of God on Horeb the mountain of God. God's presence was so sufficient for Moses that he neither needed to eat or even drink. In heaven in the presence of God, we will eat for pleasure and drink for pleasure, for we will not need to eat or drink to sustain our bodies, for the presence of God will be totally sufficient to sustain us.

Moses fed on the Word, for while he sat in God's presence he recorded the words of the covenant, the ten commandments (the WORD OF GOD).

When Moses came down he knew not that his skin shone. Moses' physical human flesh had absorbed the glory of God while he talked with God.

Absorb the Glory

IN THESE LAST DAYS God will pour out His Spirit on all flesh. Our physical human flesh can absorb the glory of God. So that we can reflect His glory. 2 Corinthians 3:18.

> *"But we all, with open face beholding as in a glass the glory of the Lord, are changed into the same image from glory to glory, even as by the Spirit of the Lord"* (2 Corinthians 3:18).

That will enable us to be able ministers of the New Covenant 2 Corinthians 3:6.

> *"Who also hath made us able ministers of the new testament; not of the letter, but of the spirit: for the letter killeth, but the spirit giveth life"* (2 Corinthians 3:6).

I encourage you to read and study and absorb the glory of the following verses of scripture. Without going into all the details here, I had a dream from the Lord, where He took me into the scripture. He told me, the scriptures, the Word rules over all creation. God and His Word are one!

> *"In the beginning was the Word, and the Word was with God, and the Word was God. The same was in*

the beginning with God. All things were made by him; and without him was not any thing made that was made. In him was life; and the life was the light of men. And the light shineth in darkness; and the darkness comprehended it not" (John 1:1-5).

In my dream, in this heavenly experience of being inside the word, I was instructed by Jesus, who was present with me, to absorb the glory of that Word.

It was like every scripture was full of faith! And I experienced this, as living, pulsating life. It was a golden bubble, of pulsating, living light! You could breathe in this faith, or this living light. The Lord told me to tell His people that they could all visit this place at any time. He said, "Tell my people that they can come to this place at any time, through meditation of My Word." He told me that all His Word is full of living faith that is designed to give His people life and healing victory! It is designed to give us peace. He went on to say, that the more time we spend in this place we can absorb the glory of this place.

Every scripture is full of faith, life and glory! As I spent time with the Lord in this scripture, I started to take the glory and faith of that scripture into my being. At the same time I was being absorbed myself, into this living, pulsating light and life. This place was full of love, because it is full of Jesus. He and His word are one!

Not only can His people visit this place as often as they want, but it is His desire that they visit here regularly. It is feeding and meditating on the Word, until they absorb the faith and the glory of that Word or scripture. They can then, or we can then walk in the light and the power of what we have absorbed.

We meditate and absorb this glory into our soul, mind, will and emotions. From there this faith and glory is absorbed down into our spirit. Once it is in our spirit or our heart, we can speak it forth from our mouth and it will manifest into our bodies, life, families and circumstances.

God's Word is alive, active and sharper than any two edged sword. Here are some verses for you to meditate on as you fast and absorb the faith and the glory that is contained in these verses.

> *"For the word of God is quick, and powerful, and sharper than any two-edged sword, piercing even to the dividing asunder of soul and spirit, and of the joints and marrow, and is a discerner of the thoughts and intents of the heart"* (Hebrews 4:12).

> *"Now faith is the substance of things hoped for, the evidence of things not seen. For by it the elders obtained a good report. Through faith we understand that the worlds were framed by the word of God, so that things which are seen were not made of things which do appear"* (Hebrews 11:1-3).

Study 2 Corinthians 3:1 through to 2 Corinthians 4:7 and 2 Corinthians 5:17.

"Do we begin again to commend ourselves? or need we, as some others, epistles of commendation to you, or letters of commendation from you? Ye are our epistle written in our hearts, known and read of all men: Forasmuch as ye are manifestly declared to be the epistle of Christ ministered by us, written not with ink, but with the Spirit of the living God; not in tables of stone, but in fleshy tables of the heart. And such trust have we through Christ to God-ward: Not that we are sufficient of ourselves to think any thing as of ourselves; but our sufficiency is of God; Who also hath made us able ministers of the new testament; not of the letter, but of the spirit: for the letter killeth, but the spirit giveth life. But if the ministration of death, written and engraven in stones, was glorious, so that the children of Israel could not stedfastly behold the face of Moses for the glory of his countenance; which glory was to be done away: How shall not the ministration of the spirit be rather glorious? For if the ministration of condemnation be glory, much more doth the ministration of righteousness exceed in glory. For even that which was made glorious had no glory in this respect, by reason of the glory that excelleth. For if that which is done away was glorious, much more that which remaineth is glorious. Seeing then that we have such hope, we use great plainness of speech: And not as Moses, which put a vail over his face, that the children of Israel could not stedfastly look to the end of that which is abolished: But their minds were blinded: for until this day remaineth the same vail untaken away in the reading of the old testament; which vail is done away in Christ. But even unto this day, when Moses is read, the vail is upon their heart. Nevertheless when it shall turn to the Lord, the vail shall be taken away. Now the Lord is that Spirit: and where the Spirit of the Lord is, there is liberty. But we all, with open face beholding as in a glass the glory of the Lord, are changed into the same image from glory to glory, even as by the Spirit of the Lord.

Therefore seeing we have this ministry, as we have received mercy, we faint not; But have renounced the hidden things of dishonesty, not walking in craftiness, nor handling the word of God deceitfully; but by manifestation of the truth commending ourselves to every man's conscience in the sight of God. But if our gospel be hid, it is hid to them that are lost: In whom the god of this world hath blinded the minds of them which believe not, lest the light of the glorious gospel of Christ, who is the image of God, should shine unto them. For we preach not ourselves, but Christ Jesus the Lord; and ourselves your servants for Jesus' sake. For God, who commanded the light to shine out of darkness, hath shined in our hearts, to give the light of the knowledge of the glory of God in the face of Jesus Christ. But we have this treasure in earthen vessels, that the excellency of the power may be of God, and not of us" (2 Corinthians 3:1-4:7).

"Therefore if any man be in Christ, he is a new creature: old things are passed away; behold, all things are become new" (2 Corinthians 5:17).

The glory will be seen on us – His Glory!

Study Isaiah 60:1-6, then Isaiah 61:1 – Isaiah 62:3.

"Arise, shine; for thy light is come, and the glory of the Lord is risen upon thee. For, behold, the darkness shall cover the earth, and gross darkness the people: but the Lord shall arise upon thee, and his glory shall be seen upon thee. And the Gentiles shall come to thy light, and kings to the brightness of thy rising. Lift up thine eyes round about, and see: all they gather themselves together, they come to thee: thy sons shall come from far, and thy daughters shall be nursed at thy side. Then thou shalt see, and flow together, and thine heart shall fear, and be enlarged; because the abundance of the sea shall be converted unto thee, the forces of the Gentiles shall come unto thee. The multitude of camels shall cover thee, the dromedaries of Midian and Ephah; all they from Sheba shall come: they shall bring gold and incense; and they shall shew forth the praises of the Lord" (Isaiah 60:1-6).

"And the glory of the Lord shall be revealed, and all flesh shall see it together: for the mouth of the Lord hath spoken it" (Isaiah 40:5).

Remember God's Word is full of God, full of faith and full of glory!

And the glory of the Lord shall be revealed, and all flesh shall see it together: for the mouth of the Lord hath spoken it.

Moses delivered the Word (which is God's Glory) to the people. Verse 32

Moses had to have a veil on his face from that time, every time he spoke to the people. But he took the veil off when he spoke to God and replaced it when he spoke to the people.

Additional Scriptures to Study

Exodus 31:18.

Exodus 32:16. The original commandments written with finger of God. Laser light coming out of the hand of God.

Habbukuk 3:4 Out of God's hand proceeds shafts of light and therein is the hiding place of His power!

Exodus 32:19. Moses broke the original tables of stone.

Exodus 32:31-32. Moses interceded for Israel.

Exodus 33:11-23. Moses.

Exodus 34:1-10.

God proclaimed His name to Moses!

We have the name of Jesus!

God through Moses and His name proclaimed to him (Exodus 34:10), did powerful miracles marvels. The people beheld these acts that changed history. God revealed His ways to Moses and His acts to the children of Israel.

How much more can we now expect God to do miracles through the name of Jesus and this better covenant built on better promises.

They were allowed no other gods before the Lord God. How much more now should we love the Lord our God and have no other gods before Him under this better covenant (Exodus 34:12-14).

Exodus 34:15-16 Old Covenant.
2 Corinthians 6:14-18 New Covenant.

Chapter Six

PROBLEM, ACTION, ANSWER

The following scriptures contain the words: chastened, proverb, humble. Below are the Hebrew meanings. Read the scriptures, meditate carefully by applying meanings, and bring your soul into line. Don't let circumstances take a hold of you, rule and reign over them. Take thoughts captive. Let faith reign and put your trust in God.

Chastened (Heb 3198), from the Stong's Concordance means – to be right, to argue, to decide, justify or convict, appoint, argue, chasten, convince, correct, daysman (intercessor), dispute, judge, maintain, plead, reason (together), rebuke, reprove, surely in any wise.

Proverb – to rule, to have power, reign, dominion, to have, superiority in mental action, a proverb.

Humble – depressed in mind or circumstances, afflicted, lonely, humble, needy, poor, heed, pay attention, to sing, shout, testify, hear, bring low, abase self, afflict, chasten self, deal hardly, exercise force, gentleness, hurt self, submit, weaken in any wise.

1. PROBLEM - ACTION - ANSWER

PROBLEM

"For my love they are my adversaries: but I give myself unto prayer" (Psalm 109:4).

Here the Psalmist was experiencing the emotional trauma of being betrayed by his friends. They had now become his enemies and were causing major problems.

ACTION

"My knees are weak through fasting; and my flesh faileth of fatness" (Psalm 109:24).

The Psalmist had taken positive action. In every situation we have a choice to make. We can react or act with the Word of God. He had chosen the latter and now was seeking comfort and victory through prayer and fasting.

ANSWER

"I will greatly praise the Lord with my mouth; yea, I will praise him among the multitude. For he shall stand at the right hand of the poor, to save him from those that condemn his soul" (Psalm 109:30-31).

Because he took positive action and prayed and fasted. Because he sought God first, putting his faith and trust in God. We see the final outcome. God sticks by his side to save him.

Be Pro Active

"When I wept, and chastened my soul with fasting, that was to my reproach. I made sackcloth also my garment; and I became a proverb to them" (Psalm 69:10-11).

"The humble shall see this, and be glad: and your heart shall live that seek God" (Psalm 69:32).

"For my love they are my adversaries: but I give myself unto prayer" (Psalm 109:4).

"My knees are weak through fasting; and my flesh faileth of fatness" (Psalm 109:24).

Supplications (Heb 8469 Strongs) - earnest prayers, entreaty, supplication, implore - asking God the superior to show favour to an inferior, to have mercy and show favour.

"Therefore go thou, and read in the roll, which thou hast written from my mouth, the words of the LORD in the ears of the people in the LORD'S house upon the fasting day: and also thou shalt read them in the ears of all Judah that come out of their cities. It may be they will present their supplication before the LORD, and will return every one from his evil way: for great is the anger and the fury that the LORD hath pronounced against this people" (Jer 36:6-7).

Fasting and reading the Word used to turn the hearts of the people away from sin and back to God.

2. PROBLEM ACTION ANSWER

PROBLEM

Because of the King's decree and Daniel's desire to please God, Daniel was placed unjustly into the lion's den.

> "Then they came near, and spake before the king concerning the king's decree; Hast thou not signed a decree, that every man that shall ask a petition of any God or man within thirty days, save of thee, O king, shall be cast into the den of lions? The king answered and said, The thing is true, according to the law of the Medes and Persians, which altereth not. Then answered they and said before the king, That Daniel, which is of the children of the captivity of Judah, regardeth not thee, O king, nor the decree that thou hast signed, but maketh his petition three times a day" (Daniel 6:12-13).

ACTION

Night of fasting, no dinner, no pleasure, no sleep.

> "Then the king went to his palace, and passed the night fasting: neither were instruments of music brought before him: and his sleep went from him" (Daniel 6:18).

ANSWER

Daniel delivered from lion's mouth.

"And when he came to the den, he cried with a lamentable voice unto Daniel: and the king spake and said to Daniel, O Daniel, servant of the living God, is thy God, whom thou servest continually, able to deliver thee from the lions? Then said Daniel unto the king, O king, live for ever. My God hath sent his angel, and hath shut the lions' mouths, that they have not hurt me: forasmuch as before him innocency was found in me; and also before thee, O king, have I done no hurt" (Daniel 6:20-22).

"He delivereth and rescueth, and he worketh signs and wonders in heaven and in earth, who hath delivered Daniel from the power of the lions. So this Daniel prospered in the reign of Darius, and in the reign of Cyrus the Persian" (Daniel 6:27-28).

After this the King dealt harshly with Daniel's enemies and promoted Daniel, who had honoured God. The King himself also acknowledged the greatness of Daniel's God.

THE FAST WAY TO POWER

CHAPTER SEVEN

DANIEL INTERCEDES ON BEHALF OF ISRAEL

"And I set my face unto the Lord God, to seek by prayer and supplications, with fasting, and sackcloth, and ashes:" (Daniel 9:3).

"And I prayed unto the LORD my God, and made my confession, and said, O Lord, the great and dreadful God, keeping the covenant and mercy to them that love him, and to them that keep his commandments (HIS WORD); We have sinned, and have committed iniquity, and have done wickedly, and have rebelled, even by departing from thy precepts and from thy judgments: Neither have we hearkened unto thy servants the prophets, which spake in thy name to our kings, our princes, and our fathers, and to all the *people of the land. O Lord, righteousness belongeth unto thee, but unto us confusion of faces, as at this day; to the men of Judah, and to the inhabitants of Jerusalem, and unto all Israel, that are near, and that are far off, through all the countries whither thou hast driven them, because of their trespass that they have trespassed against thee. O Lord, to us belongeth confusion of face, to our kings, to our princes, and to our fathers, because we have sinned against thee. To the Lord our God belong mercies and forgiveness, though we have rebelled against him; Neither have we obeyed the voice of the LORD our God, to walk in his laws, which he set before us by his servants the prophets. Yea, all Israel have transgressed thy law, even by departing, that they might not obey thy voice; therefore the curse is poured upon us, and the oath that is written in the law of Moses the servant of God, because we have sinned against him. And he hath confirmed his words, which he spake against us, and against our judges that judged us, by bringing upon us a great evil: for under the whole heaven hath not been done as hath been done upon Jerusalem. As it is written in the law of Moses, all this evil is come upon us: yet made we not our prayer before the LORD our God, that we might turn from our iniquities, and understand thy truth. Therefore hath the LORD watched upon the evil, and brought it upon us: for the LORD our God is righteous in* all his works which he doeth: for we obeyed not his voice. And now, O Lord our God, that hast brought thy people forth out of the land of Egypt with a mighty hand, and hast gotten thee renown, as at this day; we have sinned, we have done wickedly. O Lord, according to all thy righteousness, I beseech thee, let thine anger and thy fury be turned away from thy city Jerusalem, thy holy mountain: because for our sins, and for the iniquities of our fathers, Jerusalem and thy people are become a reproach to all that are about us. Now therefore, O our God, hear the prayer of thy servant, and his supplications, and cause thy face to shine upon thy sanctuary that is desolate, for the Lord's sake. O my God, incline thine ear, and hear; open thine eyes, and behold our desolations, and the city which is called by thy name: for we do not present our supplications before thee for our righteousnesses, but for thy great mercies. O Lord, hear; O Lord, forgive; O Lord, hearken and do; defer not, for thine own sake, O my God: for thy city and thy people are called by thy name. And whiles I was speaking, and praying, and confessing my sin and the sin of my people Israel, and presenting my supplication before the LORD my God for the holy mountain of my God; Yea, whiles I was speaking in prayer, even the man Gabriel, whom I had seen in the vision at the beginning, being caused to fly swiftly, touched me about the time of the evening oblation.

And he informed me, and talked with me, and said, O Daniel, I am now come forth to give thee skill and understanding. At the beginning of thy supplications the commandment came forth, and I am come to show thee; for thou art greatly beloved: therefore understand the matter, and consider the vision" (Daniel 9:4-23).

Here in these passages of scripture on the previous pages we see PROBLEM ACTION ANSWER. Let's look closer at these verses.

- v4 His Word (Daniel confessed and sought His Word).
- v5 We have sinned and departed from the Word.
- v6 Not heeded the prophets.
- v7 Separated because of trespass. Righteousness belongs to God!
- v8 Confusion has come because of sin.
- v9 To the Lord our God belong mercies and forgiveness though we have rebelled against Him.
- v10 Not obeyed, not walked in the Word.
- v11 Curse is on them because of disobedience.
- v12 Great evil because of sin.
- v13 Did not pray in order to turn and understand truth (Word).
- v14 & 15 Anger because of wickedness.
- v16 Intercession to forgive and turn situation around.
- v17 Cause face to shine - hear prayer.
- v18 Favour because of God's great mercy not our righteousness.
- v19 Forgive - we are your people called by your name.

v20 Prayer of intercession, confession of his sins and sins of people.
v21 Gabriel came.
v22 Answer received.
v23 From start of prayer, Gabriel sent forth.

As a result of Daniel's prayer the angel was sent with the ANSWER (revelation knowledge that sets the people free.)

> *"And ye shall know the truth, and the truth shall make you free"* (John 8:32).

Daniel's Fast

"In those days I Daniel was mourning three full weeks. I ate no pleasant bread, neither came flesh nor wine in my mouth, neither did I anoint myself at all, till three whole weeks were fulfilled" (Daniel 10:2-3).

"Twenty one days of fasting and praying and interceding. This was not a total fast but a partial fast. "I ate no pleasant bread, neither came flesh nor wine in my mouth, neither did I anoint myself at all, till three whole weeks were fulfilled."

"Then said he unto me, Fear not, Daniel: for from the first day that thou didst set thine heart to understand, and to chasten thyself before thy God, thy words were heard, and I am come for thy words.

But the prince of the kingdom of Persia withstood me one and twenty days: but, lo, Michael, one of the chief princes, came to help me; and I remained there with the kings of Persia.

Now I am come to make thee understand what shall befall thy people in the latter days: for yet the vision is for many days.

And when he had spoken such words unto me, I set my face toward the ground, and I became dumb.

And, behold, one like the similitude of the sons of men touched my lips: then I opened my mouth, and spake, and said unto him that stood before me, O my lord, by the vision my sorrows are turned upon me, and I have retained no strength.

For how can the servant of this my lord talk with this my lord? for as for me, straightway there remained no strength in me, neither is there breath left in me.

Then there came again and touched me one like the appearance of a man, and he strengthened me,

And said, O man greatly beloved, fear not: peace be unto thee, be strong, yea, be strong. And when he had spoken unto me, I was strengthened, and said,

> *Let my lord speak; for thou hast strengthened me. Then said he, Knowest thou wherefore I come unto thee? and now will I return to fight with the prince of Persia: and when I am gone forth, lo, the prince of Grecia shall come.*
>
> *But I will shew thee that which is noted in the scripture of truth: and there is none that holdeth with me in these things, but Michael your prince"* (Daniel 10:12-21).

From day one the answer came but spiritual warfare commenced.

A battle in heavenlies – Daniel's prayer empowered his angels. Psalm 103:20-21.

> *"Bless the Lord, ye his angels, that excel in strength, that do his commandments, hearkening unto the voice of his word. Bless ye the Lord, all ye his hosts; ye ministers of his, that do his pleasure"* (Psalm 103:20-21).

The importance of speaking God's Word can be seen here in the above verses in Psalm 103. The angels of God hearken to and obey the Word of God. When we pray in tongues, we are speaking God's Word as the Holy Spirit wills. Also, when we confess God's Word, we are declaring it out into the unseen spirit realms, where spiritual warfare is taking place.

By praying in tongues and confessing God's Word we are in actual fact giving commands of authority to the angels. We are making known to them God's will in the matters we find ourselves in. We are delivering to the angels assignments that are then carried out on our behalf by them. These angels hearken to these commands given and excel in strength over coming the powers of darkness. Through the authority of the name of Jesus and our blood covenant we have with God, through the shed blood of Jesus, we can bind Satan's power. We can cast out the devil and pull down his destructive works.

Daniel set his heart to understand. He chastened, corrected and humbled himself. He spoke God's Word.

In Daniel 10v12 The angel came because of his words.

Brought understanding revelation knowledge.

- Fasting and prayer increases angelic activity.
- Fasting and prayer increases demonic activity.
- Fasting and prayer increases spiritual awareness.
- Fasting and prayer increases visions and dreams.
- Fasting and prayer brings understanding of God's will and word.

Listen

Daniel 10:15 says, you need to have a time of silence during the fast - you need to listen.

Allow the Holy Spirit to talk and bring revelation of the Word to you.

Battles while fasting sometimes leave you no strength - we need to receive the Lord's strength. (Isaiah 40:29,30,31).

Renew Strength

Praying in tongues and confessing God's Word will renew your strength during times of fasting.

Daniel was supernaturally strengthened so he could hear and commune with God.

> Joel 2:11-32 *"The LORD shall utter his voice (His Word) before his army. Turn to God with weepings, fastings and mournings because God wants to perform His Word!"*

Deal with attitudes of your heart and humble yourself. Turn to God. He is gracious, merciful, compassionate, slow to anger and rich in love!

God wants to bless. So fast and get back to God!

> *"Let the priests, the ministers of the LORD, weep between the porch and the altar, and let them say, Spare thy people, O LORD, and give not thine heritage to reproach, that the heathen should rule over them: wherefore should they say among the people, Where is their God? Then will the LORD be jealous for his land, and pity his people"* (Joel 2:17-19).

Yes God will send answers, provisions, food, prosperity, the New wine, oil. (Joel 2:19).

We shall be satisfied, God will satisfy us therewith.

He will drive back our enemies.

Be glad and rejoice for the Lord will do great things! (Joel 2:21).

Trees will bear fruit. Vine will yield its strength. Jesus will be able to be strong once again through His people. (Joel 2:22).

Fasting and Praying will bring the latter rain on the earth. (Joel 2:23).

Study James 5:7 & Zecharaiah 10:1.

Restoration will take place. Praise and worship will take off, for God will deal wondrously. You won't be ashamed.

IT WILL HAPPEN - God's Word on the matter. (Joel 2:28)
End time harvest, miracles, signs, wonders. Pouring forth of the Spirit. Great Deliverance and Salvation. (Joel 2:28-32).

FASTING WILL BRING THE PRESENCE OF GOD!

Use wisdom in fasting.

> "Then Jesus called his disciples unto him, and said, I have compassion on the multitude, because they

continue with me now three days, and have nothing to eat: and I will not send them away fasting, lest they faint in the way" (Matthew 15:32).

Be careful, use wisdom while fasting, don't faint if you have to travel, ie driving.

"And while the day was coming on, Paul besought them all to take meat, saying, This day is the fourteenth day that ye have tarried and continued fasting, having taken nothing" (Acts 27:33).

Be sensible, eat again for health reasons. God doesn't want one hair of your head damaged.

Plan your fast, use a strategy, stick to it, don't be deceived.

"And if I send them away fasting to their own houses, they will faint by the way: for many of them came from far" (Mark 8:3).

"Defraud ye not one the other, except it be with consent for a time, that ye may give yourselves to fasting and prayer; and come together again, that Satan tempt you not for your incontinency" (1 Corinthians 7:5).

Put aside sex with your spouse for a time of prayer and fasting - for a season only, then come together again so Satan doesn't tempt you. As above - use wisdom in fasting.

Fasting and Prayer Increases Faith

> "And Jesus said unto them, Because of your unbelief: for verily I say unto you, If ye have faith as a grain of mustard seed, ye shall say unto this mountain, Remove hence to yonder place; and it shall remove; and nothing shall be impossible unto you. Howbeit this kind goeth not out but by prayer and fasting" (Matthew 17:20-21).

Faith grows - fasting and prayer increases faith and causes it to grow.

> "Jesus said unto him, If thou canst believe, all things are possible to him that believeth. And straightway the father of the child cried out, and said with tears, Lord, I believe; help thou mine unbelief. When Jesus saw that the people came running together, he rebuked the foul spirit, saying unto him, Thou dumb and deaf spirit, I charge thee, come out of him, and enter no more into him. And the spirit cried, and rent him sore, and came out of him: and he was as one dead; insomuch that many said, He is dead. But Jesus took him by the hand, and lifted him up; and he arose. And when he was come into the house, his disciples asked him privately, Why could not we cast him out? And he said unto them, This kind can come forth by nothing, but by prayer and fasting" (Mark 9:23-29).

Prayer and Fasting gets rid of unbelief and enables the power of God to work. All things are possible!

Fasting doesn't move God, it moves us into a position or attitude, a place where we can receive from God.

Remember, it is your attitude that will determine your altitude. How high do you want to fly?

From faith to faith, from glory to glory!

Works Righteousness

> *"But in every nation he that feareth him, and worketh righteousness, is accepted with him"* (Acts 10:35).

Prayer and fasting and giving for right reasons is a work of righteousness.

Declared God's full will.

> *"How God anointed Jesus of Nazareth with the Holy Ghost and with power: who went about doing good, and healing all that were oppressed of the devil; for God was with him"* (Acts 10:38).

Remember Jesus fasted and encouraged his disciples to fast oftener.

THE FAST WAY TO POWER

Chapter Eight

FASTING SUPERCHARGES PRAYER

Acts 10 says, "*There was a certain man in Caesarea called Cornelius, a centurion of the band called the Italian band, A devout man, and one that feared God with all his house, which gave much alms to the people, and prayed to God alway. He saw in a vision evidently about the ninth hour of the day an angel of God coming in to him, and saying unto him, Cornelius. And when he looked on him, he was afraid, and said, What is it, Lord? And he said unto him, Thy prayers and thine alms are come up for a memorial before God. And now send men to Joppa, and call for one Simon, whose surname is Peter: He lodgeth with one Simon a tanner, whose house is by the sea side: he shall tell thee what thou oughtest to do. And when the angel which spake unto Cornelius was departed, he called two of his household servants, and a devout soldier of them that waited on him continually; And*

when he had declared all these things unto them, he sent them to Joppa. On the morrow, as they went on their journey, and drew nigh unto the city, Peter went up upon the housetop to pray about the sixth hour: And he became very hungry, and would have eaten: but while they made ready, he fell into a trance, And saw heaven opened, and a certain vessel descending unto him, as it had been a great sheet knit at the four corners, and let down to the earth: Wherein were all manner of fourfooted beasts of the earth, and wild beasts, and creeping things, and fowls of the air. And there came a voice to him, Rise, Peter; kill, and eat. But Peter said, Not so, Lord; for I have never eaten any thing that is common or unclean. And the voice spake unto him again the second time, What God hath cleansed, that call not thou common. This was done thrice: and the vessel was received up again into heaven. Now while Peter doubted in himself what this vision which he had seen should mean, behold, the men which were sent from Cornelius had made inquiry for Simon's house, and stood before the gate, And called, and asked whether Simon, which was surnamed Peter, were lodged there. While Peter thought on the vision, the Spirit said unto him, Behold, three men seek thee. Arise therefore, and get thee down, and go with them, doubting nothing: for I have sent them. Then Peter went down to the men which were sent unto him from Cornelius; and said, Behold, I am he whom ye seek: what is the cause wherefore ye are come? And they said, Cornelius the centurion, a just man, and one that feareth God, and of good report among all the nation of the Jews, was warned from God by an holy angel to send for thee into his house, and to hear words of thee. Then called he them in, and lodged them. And on the morrow Peter went away with them, and certain brethren from Joppa accompanied him. And the morrow after they entered into Caesarea. And Cornelius waited for them, and had called together his kinsmen and near friends. And as Peter was coming in, Cornelius met him, and fell down at his feet, and worshipped him. But Peter took him up, saying, Stand up; I myself also am a man. And as he talked with him, he went in, and found many that were come together. And he said unto them, Ye know how that it is an unlawful thing for a man that is a Jew to keep company, or come unto one of another nation; but God hath showed me that I should not call any man common or unclean. Therefore came I unto you without gainsaying, as soon as I was sent for: I ask therefore for what intent ye have sent for me? And Cornelius said, Four days ago I was fasting until this hour; and at the ninth hour I prayed in my house, and, behold, a man stood before me in bright clothing, And said, Cornelius, thy prayer is heard, and thine alms are had in remembrance in the sight of God. Send therefore to Joppa, and call hither Simon, whose surname is Peter; he is lodged in the house of one Simon a tanner by the sea side: who, when he cometh, shall speak unto thee. Immediately therefore I sent to thee; and thou hast well done that thou art come. Now therefore are we all here present before God, to hear all things that are commanded thee of God. Then Peter opened his mouth, and said, Of a truth I perceive that God is no respecter of persons: But in every nation he that feareth him, and worketh righteousness, is accepted with him. The word which God sent unto the children of Israel, preaching peace by Jesus Christ: (he is Lord of all:) That word, I say, ye know, which was published throughout all Judaea, and began from Galilee, after the baptism which John preached; How God anointed Jesus of Nazareth with the Holy Ghost and with power: who went about doing good, and healing all that were oppressed of the devil; for God was with him. And we are witnesses of all things which he did both in the land of the Jews, and in Jerusalem; whom they slew and hanged on a tree: Him God raised up the third day, and showed him openly; Not to all the people, but unto witnesses chosen before of God, even to us, who did eat and drink with him after he rose from the dead. And he commanded us to preach unto the people, and to testify that it is he which was ordained of God to be the Judge of quick and dead.

To him give all the prophets witness, that through his name whosoever believeth in him shall receive remission of sins. While Peter yet spake these words, the Holy Ghost fell on all them which heard the word. And they of the circumcision which believed were astonished, as many as came with Peter, because that on the Gentiles also was poured out the gift of the Holy Ghost. For they heard them speak with tongues, and magnify God. They answered Peter, Can any man forbid water, that these should not be baptized, which have received the Holy Ghost as well as we? And he commanded them to be baptized in the name of the Lord. Then prayed they him to tarry certain days."

Cornelius - a devout man, who feared God with All his house. He taught his children in ways of God. He was a big giver, gave to poor, prayed and fasted regularly. His lifestyle of faith, combined with prayer and fasting, moved the hand of God on his behalf.

He saw a vision. His way of life opened heaven! It brought angel activity to work for him and his house. Cornelius fasted regularly. Current fast was 4 days in duration. This devotion changed things, it made a difference. It changed circumstances and opinions and opened the door for salvation to come to his house and the Gentile nations.

Peter prayed and fasted and entered the realm of the Spirit.

He got revelation knowledge, increased angel activity, brought direction, made known God's will. He heard the voice of God, heard the Spirit of God, it opened doors of ministry, caused worship. Brought the Word on the scene, brought a great outpouring, revival, salvation. Glory to God.

Fasting Releases Ministry

"And when they had ordained them elders in every church, and had prayed with fasting, they commended them to the Lord, on whom they believed" (Acts 14:23).

Through fasting and prayer, the prophets and apostles sought God's will to commission with anointing to ministry. This prayer and fasting released power in newly ordained elders.

"Thou shalt make thy prayer unto him, and he shall hear thee, and thou shalt pay thy vows. Thou shalt also decree a thing, and it shall be established unto thee: and the light shall shine upon thy ways. When men are cast down, then thou shalt say, There is lifting up; and he shall save the humble person. He shall deliver the island of the innocent: and it is delivered by the pureness of thine hands" (Job 22:27-30).

Fasting and Prayer is Service to God

"And she was a widow of about fourscore and four years, which departed not from the temple, but

served God with fastings and prayers night and day" (Luke 2:37).

In fastings often, in hunger and thirst, in watchings. To receive God's perfect will.

"In stripes, in imprisonments, in tumults, in labours, in watchings, in fastings;" (2 Corinthians 6:5).

Paul proved his ministry in watchings, in fasting, watchings -sleeplessness, listening, tuning in.

"In weariness and painfulness, in watchings often, in hunger and thirst, in fastings often, in cold and nakedness" (2 Corinthians 11:27).

To Make a Decree

"To confirm these days of Purim in their times appointed, according as Mordecai the Jew and Esther the queen had enjoined them, and as they had decreed for themselves and for their seed, the matters of the fastings and their cry" (Esther 9:31).

"Go, gather together all the Jews that are present in Shushan, and fast ye for me, and neither eat nor drink three days, night or day: I also and my maidens will fast likewise; and so will I go in unto the king, which is not according to the law: and if I perish, I perish" (Esther 4:16).

"Then I proclaimed a fast there, at the river of Ahava, that we might afflict ourselves before our God, to seek of him a right way for us, and for our little ones, and for all our substance" (Ezra 8:21).

"And Jehoshaphat feared, and set himself to seek the LORD, and proclaimed a fast throughout all Judah" (2 Chronicles 20:3).

"And she wrote in the letters, saying, Proclaim a fast, and set Naboth on high among the people:" (1 Kings 21:9).

"They proclaimed a fast, and set Naboth on high among the people" (1 Kings 21:12).

"Then said his servants unto him, What thing is this that thou hast done? thou didst fast and weep for the child, while it was alive; but when the child was dead, thou didst rise and eat bread" (2 Samuel 12:21).

Prayer and Fasting Releases Glory

"Ask ye of the LORD rain in the time of the latter rain; so the LORD shall make bright clouds (lightning), and give them showers of rain, to every one grass in the field" (Zechariah 10:1).

"...Not by might, nor by power, but by my spirit, saith the LORD of hosts" (Zechariah 4:6).

"If my people, which are called by my name, shall humble themselves, and pray, and seek my face, and turn from their wicked ways; then will I hear from heaven, and will forgive their sin, and will heal their land" (2 Chronicles 7:14).

"But ye, beloved, building up yourselves on your most holy faith, praying in the Holy Ghost" (Jude 1:20).

"Cry aloud, spare not, lift up thy voice like a trumpet, and show my people their transgression, and the house of Jacob their sins. Yet they seek me daily, and delight to know my ways, as a nation that did righteousness, and forsook not the ordinance of their God: they ask of me the ordinances of justice; they take delight in approaching to God. Wherefore have we fasted, say they, and thou seest not? wherefore have we afflicted our soul, and thou takest no knowledge? Behold, in the day of your fast ye find pleasure, and exact all your labours. Behold, ye fast for strife and debate, and to smite with the fist of wickedness: ye shall not fast as ye do this day, to make your voice to be heard on high. Is it such a fast that I have chosen? a day for a man to afflict his soul? is it to bow down his head as

a bulrush, and to spread sackcloth and ashes under him? wilt thou call this a fast, and an acceptable day to the LORD? Is not this the fast that I have chosen? to loose the bands of wickedness, to undo the heavy burdens, and to let the oppressed go free, and that ye break every yoke? Is it not to deal thy bread to the hungry, and that thou bring the poor that are cast out to thy house? when thou seest the naked, that thou cover him; and that thou hide not thyself from thine own flesh? Then shall thy light break forth as the morning, and thine health shall spring forth speedily: and thy righteousness shall go before thee; the glory of the LORD shall be thy rearward. Then shalt thou call, and the LORD shall answer; thou shalt cry, and he shall say, Here I am. If thou take away from the midst of thee the yoke, the putting forth of the finger, and speaking vanity; And if thou draw out thy soul to the hungry, and satisfy the afflicted soul; then shall thy light rise in obscurity, and thy darkness be as the noon day: And the LORD shall guide thee continually, and satisfy thy soul in drought, and make fat thy bones: and thou shalt be like a watered garden, and like a spring of water, whose waters fail not. And they that shall be of thee shall build the old waste places: thou shalt raise up the foundations of many generations; and thou shalt be called, The repairer of the breach, The restorer of paths to dwell in. If thou turn away thy foot from the sabbath, from doing *thy pleasure on my holy day; and call the sabbath a delight, the holy of the LORD, honourable; and shalt honour him, not doing thine own ways, nor finding thine own pleasure, nor speaking thine own words: Then shalt thou delight thyself in the LORD; and I will cause thee to ride upon the high places of the earth, and feed thee with the heritage of Jacob thy father: for the mouth of the LORD hath spoken it"* (Isaiah 58).

The Hebrew word for glory, in the above verses is an interesting word. It means that as we pray and fast to release God's glory, this glory as our rearward will gather up results for us. Producing abundance and riches. It brings honour, splendour and God's glory into the external conditions and circumstances.

Humility

"When they fast, I will not hear their cry; and when they offer burnt offering and an oblation, I will not accept them: but I will consume them by the sword, and by the famine, and by the pestilence" (Jeremiah 14:12).

Fasting to God to hear their cry, but to no avail because of sin. Must deal with sin and repent.

"And it came to pass in the fifth year of Jehoiakim the son of Josiah king of Judah, in the ninth month, that

> they proclaimed a fast before the LORD to all the people in Jerusalem, and to all the people that came from the cities of Judah unto Jerusalem" (Jeremiah 36:9).

After God's warnings, they fasted and read God's word.

> "Sanctify ye a fast, call a solemn assembly, gather the elders and all the inhabitants of the land into the house of the LORD your God, and cry unto the LORD" (Joel 1:14).

Sanctify a fast and pray - all the people.

> "So the people of Nineveh believed God, and proclaimed a fast, and put on sackcloth, from the greatest of them even to the least of them" (Jonah 3:5).

All the people believed the Word. They repented, prayed, turned from their evil ways and fasted.

> "And he prayed unto the LORD, and said, I pray thee, O LORD, was not this my saying, when I was yet in my country? Therefore I fled before unto Tarshish: for I knew that thou art a gracious God, and merciful, slow to anger, and of great kindness, and repentest thee of the evil" (Jonah 4:2).

Their fasting, seeking and praying brought upon them God's grace, mercy. They experienced a revival at that time involving approximately 120,000 people.

> *"Speak unto all the people of the land, and to the priests, saying, When ye fasted and mourned in the fifth and seventh month, even those seventy years, did ye at all fast unto me, even to me?"* (Zechariah 7:5).

Fast unto God

When we fast, it is a time of realigning ourselves to God's will and purpose for our life.

> *"Thus saith the LORD of hosts; The fast of the fourth month, and the fast of the fifth, and the fast of the seventh, and the fast of the tenth, shall be to the house of Judah joy and gladness, and cheerful feasts; therefore love the truth and peace"* (Zechariah 8:19).

As a result of the above times of fasting, love, truth and peace came to the house of Judah. This joy and gladness and obedience to God brought the people revival. God was with them as a result of their fasting and turning their lives back to God, His will and ways.

> *"Thus saith the Lord of hosts; In those days it shall come to pass, that ten men shall take hold out of all languages of the nations, even shall take hold of the*

> skirt of him that is a Jew, saying, We will go with you: for we have heard that God is with you" (Zechariah 8:23).

> "Moreover when ye fast, be not, as the hypocrites, of a sad countenance: for they disfigure their faces, that they may appear unto men to fast. Verily I say unto you, They have their reward" (Matthew 6:16).

Keep fasting a secret to receive an open reward from God. Wash, be glad, look good, press in!

> "But lay up for yourselves treasures in heaven, where neither moth nor rust doth corrupt, and where thieves do not break through nor steal:" (Matthew 6:20).

Lays up treasure in heaven.

> "The light of the body is the eye: if therefore thine eye be single, thy whole body shall be full of light" (Matthew 6:22).

Fasting fills the body with light.

> "But seek ye first the kingdom of God, and his righteousness; and all these things shall be added unto you" (Matthew 6:33).

Scriptural fasting seeks God first!

> "Then came to him the disciples of John, saying, Why do we and the Pharisees fast oft, but thy disciples fast not? And Jesus said unto them, Can the children of the bridechamber mourn, as long as the bridegroom is with them? but the days will come, when the bridegroom shall be taken from them, and then shall they fast" (Matthew 9:14-15).

As a new creation can hold the new wine. When we fast we empty ourselves to be filled. Disciples were not yet ready to fast to be filled up with new wine. They had to be born again to be new bottles first, so as to contain the new wine (the fullness of the Holy Spirit).

> "And the disciples of John and of the Pharisees used to fast: and they come and say unto him, Why do the disciples of John and of the Pharisees fast, but thy disciples fast not? And Jesus said unto them, Can the children of the bridechamber fast, while the bridegroom is with them? as long as they have the bridegroom with them, they cannot fast. But the days will come, when the bridegroom shall be taken away from them, and then shall they fast in those days. No man also seweth a piece of new cloth on an old garment: else the new piece that filled it up taketh away from the old, and the rent is made worse. And no man putteth new wine into old bottles: else the new wine doth burst the bottles, and the wine is spilled, and the bottles will be marred: but new wine must be put into new bottles" (Mark 2:18-22).

New wine in new bottles.

> *"And they said unto him, Why do the disciples of John fast often, and make prayers, and likewise the disciples of the Pharisees; but thine eat and drink? And he said unto them, Can ye make the children of the bridechamber fast, while the bridegroom is with them? But the days will come, when the bridegroom shall be taken away from them, and then shall they fast in those days"* (Luke 5:33-35).

Jesus' disciples will fast often and make prayers often. Through fasting, we keep ourselves refreshed and renewed, ready to receive the new wine.

> *"And be not drunk with wine, wherein is excess; but be filled with the Spirit"* (Ephesians 5:18).

Pharisees regularly fasted twice in a week but to no avail because of pride. Their motives were wrong. They needed an attitude adjustment, in order to receive the benefits of their fast.

> *"I fast twice in the week, I give tithes of all that I possess"* (Luke 18:12).

We must repent of sins when we fast.

> *"Now when much time was spent, and when sailing was now dangerous, because the fast was now already past, Paul admonished them"* (Acts 27:9).

We always have to look at ourselves, judge ourselves and make the necessary adjustments to our attitudes and lives. A time of fasting and seeking God is always a good time to bring ourselves back into alignment with God's will for our life.

Special Fast Day

> *"And the LORD spake unto Moses, saying, Also on the tenth day of this seventh month there shall be a day of atonement: it shall be an holy convocation unto you; and ye shall afflict your souls, and offer an offering made by fire unto the LORD. And ye shall do no work in that same day: for it is a day of atonement, to make an atonement for you before the LORD your God. For whatsoever soul it be that shall not be afflicted in that same day, he shall be cut off from among his people"* (Leviticus 23:26-29).

One day to fast and make offerings, do no work. It was to be a time of rest from one evening until the next.

> "Then all the children of Israel, and all the people, went up, and came unto the house of God, and wept, and sat there before the LORD, and fasted that day until even, and offered burnt offerings and peace offerings before the LORD" (Judges 20:26).

One day fast by all the people for deliverance out of the hand of the enemy.

> *"And they gathered together to Mizpeh, and drew water, and poured it out before the LORD, and fasted on that day, and said there, We have sinned against the LORD. And Samuel judged the children of Israel in Mizpeh"* (1 Samuel 7:6).

One day fast because of sin. Samuel intercedes. Pouring out water (symbolic of tongues, in intercession, praying.)

Seven Day Fast

> *"And they took their bones, and buried them under a tree at Jabesh, and fasted seven days"* (1 Samuel 31:13).

> *"And they mourned, and wept, and fasted until even, for Saul, and for Jonathan his son, and for the people of the LORD, and for the house of Israel; because they were fallen by the sword"* (2 Samuel 1:12).

All the people mourned, wept and fasted.

> *"So David waxed greater and greater: for the LORD of hosts was with him"* (1 Chronicles 11:9).

> *"David therefore besought God for the child; and David fasted, and went in, and lay all night upon the earth"* (2 Samuel 12:16).

He besought God - lay on the earth, fasting and praying.

> "And he said, While the child was yet alive, I fasted and wept: for I said, Who can tell whether GOD will be gracious to me, that the child may live?" (2 Samuel 12:22).

David fasted for miracle healing breakthrough. Wept - intercession.

> "And it came to pass, when Ahab heard those words, that he rent his clothes, and put sackcloth upon his flesh, and fasted, and lay in sackcloth, and went softly" (1 Kings 21:27).

Your attitude of humility, repentance will be witnessed by God.

> "They arose, all the valiant men, and took away the body of Saul, and the bodies of his sons, and brought them to Jabesh, and buried their bones under the oak in Jabesh, and fasted seven days" (1 Chronicles 10:12).

> "So we fasted and besought our God for this: and he was intreated of us" (Ezra 8:23).

Fasted for protection and direction - gave an offering.

> "And it came to pass, when I heard these words, that I sat down and wept, and mourned certain days, and fasted, and prayed before the God of heaven" (Nehemiah 1:4).

Nehemiah interceded on behalf of the people to God, to rebuild, to forgive and to have mercy. The result was the city and wall were rebuilt.

God is merciful, He wants to heal, forgive and make new.

> *"Speak unto all the people of the land, and to the priests, saying, When ye fasted and mourned in the fifth and seventh month, even those seventy years, did ye at all fast unto me, even to me?"* (Zechariah 7:5).

Our fast must be unto God.

> *"And when he had fasted forty days and forty nights, he was afterward an hungred"* (Matthew 4:2).

Jesus fasted 40 days and 40 nights.

The Early Elders Fasted

Ordination by fasting and prayer.

> *"As they ministered to the Lord, and fasted, the Holy Ghost said, Separate me Barnabas and Saul for the work whereunto I have called them. And when they had fasted and prayed, and laid their hands on them, they sent them away"* (Acts 13:2 & 3).

Fasting, prayer and giving of alms is service to God.

"Take heed that ye do not your alms before men, to be seen of them: otherwise ye have no reward of your Father which is in heaven. Therefore when thou doest thine alms, do not sound a trumpet before thee, as the hypocrites do in the synagogues and in the streets, that they may have glory of men. Verily I say unto you, They have their reward. But when thou doest alms, let not thy left hand know what thy right hand doeth: That thine alms may be in secret: and thy Father which seeth in secret himself shall reward thee openly. And when thou prayest, thou shalt not be as the hypocrites are: for they love to pray standing in the synagogues and in the corners of the streets, that they may be seen of men. Verily I say unto you, They have their reward. But thou, when thou prayest, enter into thy closet, and when thou hast shut thy door, pray to thy Father which is in secret; and thy Father which seeth in secret shall reward thee openly. But when ye pray, use not vain repetitions, as the heathen do: for they think that they shall be heard for their much speaking. Be not ye therefore like unto them: for your Father knoweth what things ye have need of, before ye ask him. After this manner therefore pray ye: Our Father which art in heaven, Hallowed be thy name. Thy kingdom come. Thy will be done in earth, as it is in heaven. Give us this day our daily bread. And forgive us our debts, as we forgive our debtors. And lead us not into temptation, but deliver us from evil: For thine is the kingdom, and the power, and the glory, for ever. Amen. For if ye forgive men their trespasses, your heavenly Father will also forgive you: But if ye forgive not men their trespasses, neither will your Father forgive your trespasses. Moreover when ye fast, be not, as the hypocrites, of a sad countenance: for they disfigure their faces, that they may appear unto men to fast. Verily I say unto you, They have their reward. But thou, when thou fastest, anoint thine head, and wash thy face; That thou appear not unto men to fast, but unto thy Father which is in secret: and thy Father, which seeth in secret, shall reward thee openly. Lay not up for yourselves treasures upon earth, where moth and rust doth corrupt, and where thieves break through and steal: But lay up for yourselves treasures in heaven, where neither moth nor rust doth corrupt, and where thieves do not break through nor steal: For where your treasure is, there will your heart be also. The light of the body is the eye: if therefore thine eye be single, thy whole body shall be full of light. But if thine eye be evil, thy whole body shall be full of darkness. If therefore the light that is in thee be darkness, how great is that darkness! No man can serve two masters: for either he will hate the one, and love the other; or else he will hold to the one, and despise the other. Ye cannot serve God and mammon" (Matthew 6:1-24).

The Prophets Fasted

"Now there were in the church that was at Antioch certain prophets and teachers; as Barnabas, and Simeon that was called Niger, and Lucius of Cyrene, and Manaen, which had been brought up with Herod the tetrarch, and Saul. As they ministered to the Lord, and fasted, the Holy Ghost said, Separate me Barnabas and Saul for the work whereunto I have called them. And when they had fasted and prayed, and laid their hands on them, they sent them away" (Acts 13:1-3).

"And there was one Anna, a prophetess, the daughter of Phanuel, of the tribe of Aser: she was of a great age, and had lived with an husband seven years from her virginity; And she was a widow of about fourscore and four years, which departed not from the temple, but served God with fastings and prayers night and day" (Luke 2:36-37).

Fasting is Service to God

Anna - prophetess served God with fastings and prayer.

"And when they had preached the gospel to that city, and had taught many, they returned again to Lystra, and to Iconium, and Antioch, Confirming the souls of the disciples, and exhorting them to continue in

> the faith, and that we must through much tribulation enter into the kingdom of God. And when they had ordained them elders in every church, and had prayed with fasting, they commended them to the Lord, on whom they believed" (Acts 14:21-23).

Fast to renew wineskin to contain new wine. WE NEED NEW WINE!

> "And Jesus said unto them, Can the children of the bridechamber mourn, as long as the bridegroom is with them? but the days will come, when the bridegroom shall be taken from them, and then shall they fast. No man putteth a piece of new cloth unto an old garment, for that which is put in to fill it up taketh from the garment, and the rent is made worse. Neither do men put new wine into old bottles: else the bottles break, and the wine runneth out, and the bottles perish: but they put new wine into new bottles, and both are preserved" (Matthew 9:15,16,17).

Paul listed fasting as one of the proofs he was a minister.

> "Are they ministers of Christ? (I speak as a fool) I am more; in labours more abundant, in stripes above measure, in prisons more frequent, in deaths oft. Of the Jews five times received I forty stripes save one. Thrice was I beaten with rods, once was I stoned, thrice I suffered shipwreck, a night and a day I have

been in the deep; In journeyings often, in perils of waters, in perils of robbers, in perils by mine own countrymen, in perils by the heathen, in perils in the city, in perils in the wilderness, in perils in the sea, in perils among false brethren; In weariness and painfulness, in watchings often, in hunger and thirst, in fastings often, in cold and nakedness. Beside those things that are without, that which cometh upon me daily, the care of all the churches"* (2 Corinthians 11:23-28).

We are commanded to imitate him as he imitated Christ.

"Be ye followers of me, even as I also am of Christ" (1 Corinthians 11:1).

Fasting humbles the soul.

"But as for me, when they were sick, my clothing was sackcloth: I humbled my soul with fasting; and my prayer returned into mine own bosom" (Psalm 35:13).
"When I wept, and chastened my soul with fasting, that was to my reproach" (Psalm 69:10).

Fasting then chastens the soul, to make adjustments and corrections in our lives, attitudes and motives. Putting us into a place to be filled again with the will, purposes and desires of God for our lives.

"Then I proclaimed a fast there, at the river of Ahava, that we might afflict ourselves before our God, to seek of him a right way for us, and for our little ones, and for all our substance." "So we fasted and besought our God for this: and he was intreated of us" (Ezra 8:21 & 23).

When done correctly the prayers of a humble person are more likely to be heard.

Chapter Nine

A TWENTY-THREE DAY FAST FOR REVIVAL
(The following chapter was taken from Gordon Lindsay's book, 'Prayer and Fasting' used by permission.)

The following is the story of a 23-day fast by Col. Len Jones, a former chaplain in the Australian armed forces. We believe this day-by day account for the fast by this Australian editor and evangelist will give much information and insight into the proper way to fast. It will also show some of the results of such a fast.

This is a diary of a 23-day fast. There is one thing God has against fasting, and He has the same against prayer and almsgiving, and that is that we do it "to be seen of men," and to glory in what we do before others. For that reason I am hesitant in putting the experience on paper. But as I read the Scriptures of the many testimonies of fasting, I am made to feel it is God's will for this experience to be made known. That convinces me that there is a place in which we can give fasting testimony, not to receive honour from men, but to bring blessings to others.

This was a complete fast. No food was taken during the fast. Only water was taken. During the time of the fast, I was conducting evangelistic meetings every night except Monday, and two meetings on Sunday. I remained in South Africa one year and during that time thousands knelt at the altar for salvation, restoration, healing and consecration of their lives afresh for the service of the Lord.

THE NEED IN SOUTH AFRICA –CAUSE OF THE FAST

When I arrived in South Africa, the whole union opened up to me for evangelistic campaigns, but I felt totally inadequate for the situation. I was conscious of a tremendous spiritual need – first, for a much deeper experience with God myself, and second, for a ministry for this country.

Something had to be done! The need was desperate! I was brought up against a brick wall – unless God met me I knew I would be a failure. Praying alone did not seem to make the slightest impression upon the burden – I could see no other way out but to fast and pray. It was a call of God! It was my only hope!

I did not know how long I would fast – I did not make a decision. I have found it wiser to start that way, for if you make a time and do not continue until that time, there can be a sense of frustration that might mar a little of the great blessings received.

1st Day – Hardest of All

Everything was black and hopeless! It was a miserable day! The first day is generally the hardest of all. Most of the day was spent in prayer – such conditions often lead you to prayer.

2nd Day – First Blessing Received

Today I felt brighter in spirit and more confident. I was not very hungry, but drank quite a lot of water. It is good to drink plenty of water while fasting. I felt weak, but this is exactly as I expected, for this is generally such during the first three days of fasting, and explains why Jesus said when He fed the four thousand, "I have compassion on the multitude, because they have now been with Me three days, and have nothing to eat: And if I send them away fasting to their own houses, they will faint on the way: for divers of them came from afar" (Mk. 8:2,3 KJV).

During the day, I was very conscious of the presence of the Lord and His blessing and peace, and in the early hours of the morning had a mighty time with God in prayer. The Lord gave me faith that all the many things being prayed for would be answered – this was a wonderful and powerful time of intercession.

3rd Day – Weakness Felt

I felt weak this morning, as was to be expected. My tongue was coated and there was a bad taste in my mouth. In the afternoon, I walked about four miles, visiting and praying. In the evening I had a wonderful meeting with the power of God in evidence.

4th Day

This evening had a wonderful meeting, when the subject was "Faith." The whole congregation was at the altar for prayer. Let me say here, that if this time of prayer and fasting was stopped right now, the services we have been having, have been more than worth it all.

5th Day – Weakness Begins to Leave

Today I was very bright in spirit and body. The feeling of weakness and lassitude that I have had during the first few days has gone and I feel fine.

The meeting in the evening was best yet. Who says that fasting as well as praying is not abundantly worthwhile?

6th Day – Blessings Increase

As I awoke this morning, I felt better and stronger than I have since I started fasting.

Today is Sunday and I have two meetings. What a wonderful meeting it was this morning. Right from the start the presence and power of God was on the meeting. Without invitation many came to the front for prayer. Physically, I felt a lassitude and weakness today with the long meetings. But with it all, I felt so restful and peaceful with steady confidence in God.

7th Day – Prayer Necessary

Today I realized afresh it must be fasting and prayer, and not fasting alone. Both are necessary!

At the end of the first week I weighed myself and found that I had lost about twelve pounds, which is about right. You lose much more the first week than later. As the fast proceeds, it generally works out at a loss of weight of about one pound a day.

8th Day – Some Physical Reaction

When I awoke this morning, there was more physical distress, but it is this that constrains you to prayer. There was a feeling of dizziness but the blessings were wonderful. There was such a peace and confidence and I felt I had such a grip of things – I felt I could meet anyone with ease and with authority. In the spirit, also, all was well - it seemed that I had vacated from the natural into the spiritual and it was wonderful.

And after all, the physical inconvenience should be expected. The natural must decrease while the spiritual increases. Daniel did not have an easy time with his 21-day fast. Scripture says he was in mourning the whole time (Dan. 10:2). Daniel says, "There remained no strength in me: for my comeliness was turned in me into corruption, and I retained no strength" (Dan. 10:8 KJV). (Also read experience of the Psalmist, Psalm 109:23-25.) And so it is with us! But Daniel and David had a wonderful spiritual experience.

Today I start a campaign in another church, and had to go stay with new people. One of the biggest trials in fasting is the people with whom we live, especially those who love us and are dear to us – they get so concerned about us.

The tendency to quit came over me this morning. "The Lord had blessed and answered my prayer. Perhaps this is enough." In the afternoon I felt so much brighter and wondered why I had ever considered ending the fast. There are moods and changes in fasting. Watch and pray!

9th Day

This was a busy day and I was on my feet most of the morning. Feeling very well in body and happy in the Lord. Preached with much blessing tonight.

10th Day – Self-examination

Just as my body has been objecting to the elimination of toxins, poisons, accumulated waste matter and other things that offend, and bids me to stop the fast, so now I am finding my spirit is objecting to the elimination of things that are displeasing to God, and bids me quit.

This is a fight to the death of everything in me (spiritual and physical) that is contrary to the will of God. And what a fight it is. How the spirit is resisting. There is no mistaking it when God shows you yourself – it takes away all your self-righteousness all right. What a fight is going on as these things lift their ugly heads, but they have to go in the same way as things that offend physically have to go.

In a time of prayer and fasting you see yourself as others see you and as God sees you. This affords you an excellent opportunity to confess and deal with all such things. As the fasting continues I am expecting other things to come up – I am also expecting that they will be dealt with.

11th Day

All is going well spiritually and physically. I feel that I am taking a vacation in heaven. Physically there is nothing like the discomfort there was a week ago. Many others are being blessed and encouraged to fast and pray. A great work has been done. Tonight, feeling that the fast has served a wonderful purpose there is a strong desire to cease. But not only am I prepared to cease, I am prepared to carry on if that is God's plan.

12th Day – New Strength Comes

Today has been a very easy day. All who have fasted, testify of the feeling of weakness, nausea and lassitude that you have the first few days and which continues up to the first week. All goes as you get around the twelfth and thirteenth day. In fact, and I know that only those who have fasted will believe me when I say it, around the fourteenth day you actually get stronger as the time goes on.

13th Day – Selfishness Revealed

Today the Lord has been dealing with me again about greed, covetousness and selfishness. As I have seen myself I seem to have been such a selfish person, always concerned about my interests – interests in God's work, yes, but also very much interested in my own needs and comforts. What a time I have had this morning! I have been low before the Lord! And then there is another great battle, closely allied to pride – wanting to be somebody in the eyes of men, wanting to impress, a hesitance to take a humble place, and being more concerned with what man thinks of your ministry than what the Lord thinks. And so these two battles were fought today in intense earnestness, with a keen desire that my heart shall be laid bare before God and that a new experience will be my portion.

What a time we had in the meeting last night, and again this morning. Many testified of healing as a result of prayer for them last night. Oh that people would pray and fast – what a difference it makes, both in regards to our own lives and ministry. It is worth it a thousand times and brings blessings that nothing else can bring.

14th Day

Today I was on my feet all through the day until 4.00pm. How well and strong I feel! It is always unbelievable, that one actually gets strong, when they pass into the third week. Only those who have experienced it will believe it! To others, it must sound like exaggeration. But how well in spirit one feels, for this time of prayer and fasting is primarily a consecration fast unto the Lord.

A week ago in the morning, as I packed my suitcase in preparation for a move to this present home, I was very weak. As I packed I had to sit down and rest, but tonight, although at the end of a very busy day, there is no feeling of weakness. It is simply amazing.

17th Day -- Great Faith Being Born

Today I feel wonderful. Fasting is no trial now, and the days come and go beautifully and easily. Spiritually, I feel that I am in another world. It is a wonderful experience and the end is not yet. I believe as the fast continues, I am going to get to that place with God that my soul has been longing. A man came to the house today to be prayed for with pains in the stomach. I felt such faith as I put my hands on him. He was healed instantly and went away rejoicing. This is happening continually in the meetings night after night.

18th Day -- Healing Ministry Being Developed

This was not such a good day. I went to the meeting with the conviction that I had not sought God sufficiently this day – yes, it is to be prayer as well as fasting. But as soon as I started to preach all tiredness left me. After I had prayed for many sick people I felt better than I had felt all day. It was encouraging tonight to hear about a dozen testify that they were healed when they were prayed for the night before.

19th Day

Today I had an attack in my body of a trouble from the days in the army, probably through army food and conditions. I am glad that it came up at this time as it enabled me to do some real praying about it.

20th Day – Increasing Blessing

What wonderful meetings we are having. A great crowd gathered last night in the city hall. Many testified in this morning's meeting of instantaneous deliverance from all kinds of troubles.

Today I preached in a way that I have seldom preached before. I seemed to have faith to believe for almost anything. Well, we are fulfilling the conditions: "Nothing shall be impossible unto you. Howbeit, this kind goeth not out but by prayer and fasting" (Matt. 17:20,21 KJV). When you are fasting, you feel that you have done the last thing and there is nothing more you can do -- it seems to give you a claim on God for the supernatural to happen.

Everyone is rejoicing at the blessing and presence of the Lord in our midst. Never do I remember being so completely concerned about the will of God only! Never did everything outside God's will seem so uninteresting and uninviting.

21st Day

One of the purposes of this fast was to encourage others to fast and pray, and to convince, by example, that no bodily harm would result. As people see me preaching night after night, looking little different than when I started, it is inspiring many others to fast and pray.

23rd Day – Fasting Ends

The appetite we have for food is very often from habit, and is not a true habit but a perverted one. Just like a heavy smoker would rather have a smoke than a meal – he has an appetite, a very real appetite, for it, but it is not a true need. This false appetite for food goes after about three days. It is not till many days later that the real appetite comes.

It is then that fasting finishes and starvation begins. This is the time to cease. It is at this time your tongue clears, your mouth and breath sweeten, and weakness returns. That is why we read about Jesus, "And when He had fasted forty days and forty nights, He was afterward an hungred" (Matt. 4:2 KJV), which suggested that He had not been hungry before.

Two or three days ago, I remarked about a new colour in my face and today my tongue, mouth and breath are sweet. And with this I have a ravenous hunger. For this reason I have decided this afternoon to finish my fast... Weighing myself at the close of the fast, I found I weighed 149 pounds compared to 176 pounds at the beginning, or a loss of 27 pounds in twenty-three days.

Breaking the Fast

It is obvious that after so long without food, the utmost care must be taken in breaking the fast. This cannot be over emphasized – the longer you fast, the more care must be exercised. Impatience here can cause much harm!

It is good to break such a fast as this with fruit juices diluted one to three – any fruit juice will do, but orange juice is best. The first day take a half glass of orange juice diluted with water, three or four times during the whole day. Double this amount the second day (it is best to take it warm). The third day drink the orange juice undiluted. Perhaps a little fruit may be taken. On the fourth day you can take several meals of fresh fruit. On the fifth day take a half pint of milk every two hours. On the sixth day you can begin eating meals of raw vegetables such as tomatoes, carrots and lettuce. From now on you can gradually work back to your usual diet.

Breaking your fast is more difficult than the fast itself. You will certainly be a very unwise person and will risk serious damage, which could prove fatal, if you unduly rush this breaking of the fast period.

With all my heart I thank God for the past twenty-three days. Words fail to express the blessings I have received both spiritually and physically, and I believe the results of the fast which follow will be even greater than the results during the fast have been.

CHAPTER TEN

SEVEN BASIC STEPS TO SUCCESSFUL
FASTING & PRAYER

How To Begin Your Fast

How you begin and conduct your fast will largely determine your success. By following these seven basic steps to fasting, you will make your time with the Lord more meaningful and spiritually rewarding.

STEP 1: SET YOUR OBJECTIVE

Why are you fasting? Is it for spiritual renewal, for guidance, for healing, for the resolution of problems, for special grace to handle a difficult situation? Ask the Holy Spirit to clarify His leading and objectives for your prayer fast. This will enable you to pray more specifically and strategically.

Through fasting and prayer, we humble ourselves before God, so the Holy Spirit will stir our souls, awaken our churches, and heal our land according to 2 Chronicles 7:14.

Make this a priority in your fasting.

STEP 2: MAKE YOUR COMMITMENT

Pray about the kind of fast you should undertake. Jesus implied that all of His followers should fast (Matthew 6:16-18; 9:14,15). For Him it was a matter of when believers would fast, not if they would do it. Before you fast, decide the following up front:

- How long you will fast – one meal, one day, a week, several weeks, forty days (Beginners should start slowly, building up to longer fasts.)
- The type of fast God wants you to undertake (such as water only, or water and juices; what kinds of juices you will drink and how often.)
- What physical or social activities you will restrict.
- How much time each day you will devote to prayer and God's Word.

Making these commitments ahead of time, will help you sustain your fast, when physical temptations and life's pressures tempt you to abandon it.

STEP 3: PREPARE YOURSELF SPIRITUALLY

The very foundation of fasting and prayer is repentance. Unconfessed sin will hinder your prayers. Here are several things you can do to prepare your heart:

- Ask God to help you make a comprehensive list of your sins.
- Confess every sin that the Holy Spirit calls to your

remembrance and accept God's forgiveness (1 John 1:9).
- Seek forgiveness from all whom you have offended, and forgive all who have hurt you (Mark 11:25; Luke 11:4; 17:3,4).
- Make restitution as the Holy Spirit leads you.
- Ask God to fill you with His Holy Spirit according to His command in Ephesians 5:18 and His promise in 1 John 5:14,15.
- Surrender your life fully to Jesus Christ as your Lord and Master; refuse to obey your worldly nature (Romans 12:1,2).
- Meditate on the attributes of God, His love, sovereignty, power, wisdom, faithfulness, grace, compassion, and others (Psalm 48:9,10; 103:1-8, 11-13).
- Begin your time of fasting and prayer with an expectant heart (Hebrews 11:6).
- Do not underestimate spiritual opposition. Satan sometimes intensifies the natural battle between body and spirit (Galatians 5:16,17).

STEP 4: PREPARE YOURSELF PHYSICALLY

Fasting requires reasonable precautions. Consult your physician first, especially if you take prescription medication or have a chronic ailment. Some persons should never fast without professional supervision.

Physical preparation makes the drastic change in your eating routine a little easier so that you can turn your full attention to the Lord in prayer.
- Do not rush into your fast.

- Prepare your body. Eat smaller meals before starting a fast. Avoid high-fat and sugary foods.
- Eat raw fruit and vegetables for two days before starting a fast.

While You Fast

Your time of fasting and prayer has come. You are abstaining from all solid foods and have begun to seek the Lord. Here are some helpful suggestions to consider:

- Avoid drugs, even natural herbal drugs and homeopathic remedies. Medication should be withdrawn only with your physician's supervision.
- Limit your activity.
- Exercise moderately. Walk one to three kilometers or miles each day if convenient and comfortable.
- Rest as much as your schedule will permit.
- Prepare yourself for temporary mental discomforts, such as impatience, crankiness and anxiety.
- Expect some physical discomforts, especially on the second day. You may have fleeting hunger pains, dizziness, or the "blahs." Withdrawal from caffeine and sugar may cause headaches. Physical annoyances may also include weakness, tiredness, or sleeplessness.

The first two or three days are usually the hardest. As you continue to fast, you will likely experience a sense of well-being both physically and spiritually. However, should you feel hunger pains, increase your liquid intake.

STEP 5: PUT YOURSELF ON A SCHEDULE

For maximum spiritual benefit, set aside ample time to be alone with the Lord. Listen for His leading. The more time you spend with Him, the more meaningful your fast will be.

Morning
- Begin your day in praise and worship.
- Read and meditate on God's Word, preferably on your knees.
- Invite the Holy Spirit to work in you to will and to do His good pleasure according to Philippians 2:13.
- Invite God to use you. Ask Him to show you how to influence your world, your family, your church, your community, your country, and beyond.
- Pray for His vision for your life and empowerment to do His will.

Noon
- Return to prayer and God's Word.
- Take a short prayer walk.
- Spend time in intercessory prayer for your community's and nation's leaders, for the world's unreached millions, for your family or special needs.

Evening
- Get alone for an unhurried time of "seeking His face."
- If others are fasting with you, meet together for prayer.
- Avoid television or any other distraction that may dampen your spiritual focus.

When possible, begin and end each day on your knees with your spouse for a brief time of praise and thanksgiving to God. Longer periods of time with our Lord in prayer and study of His Word are often better spent alone.

Suggested Schedules

A dietary routine is vital as well. Dr Julio C Ruibal – a nutritionist, pastor, and specialist in fasting and prayer – suggests a daily schedule and list of juices you may find useful and satisfying. Modify this schedule and the drinks you take to suit your circumstances and tastes.

5 am – 8 am
Fruit juices, preferably freshly squeezed or blended and diluted in 50 percent distilled water if the fruit is acid. Apple, pear, grapefruit, papaya, watermelon, or other fruit juices are generally preferred. If you cannot do your own juicing, buy juices without sugar or additives.

10:30 am – noon
Fresh vegetable juice made from lettuce, celery, and carrots in three equal parts.

2:30 pm – 4 pm
Herb tea with a drop of honey. Avoid black tea or any tea with caffeine.

6 pm – 8:30 pm
Broth made from boiling potatoes, celery, and carrots with no salt. After boiling about half an hour, pour the contents into a container and drink it.

Tips on Juice Fasting:
- Drinking fruit juice will decrease your hunger pains and give you some natural sugar energy. The taste and lift will motivate and strengthen you to continue.

- The best juices are made from fresh watermelon, lemons, grapes, apples, cabbage, beets, carrots, celery, or leafy green vegetables. In cold weather, you may enjoy a warm vegetable broth.
- Mix acidic juices (orange and tomato) with water for your stomach's sake.
- Avoid caffeinated drinks. Avoid chewing gum or mints, even if your breath is bad. They stimulate digestive action in your stomach.

Breaking Your Fast

When your designated time for fasting is finished, you will begin to eat again. But how you break your fast is extremely important for your physical and spiritual well-being.

STEP 6: END YOUR FAST GRADUALLY

Begin eating gradually. Do not eat solid foods immediately after your fast. Suddenly reintroducing solid food to your stomach and digestive tract will likely have negative, even dangerous, consequences. Try several smaller meals or snacks each day. If you end your fast gradually, the beneficial physical and spiritual effects will result in continued good health.

Here are some suggestions to help you end your fast properly:
- Break an extended fast with fruit such as watermelon.
- While continuing to drink fruit or vegetable juices, add the following:
  First day: Add a raw salad.
  Second day: Add baked potato, no butter or seasoning.
  Third day: Add steamed vegetables.

Thereafter: Begin to reintroduce your normal diet.
- Gradually return to regular eating with several small snacks during the first few days. Start with a little soup and fresh fruit such as watermelon and cantaloupe. Advance to a few tablespoons of solid foods such as raw fruits and vegetables or a raw salad and baked potato.

A Final Word

STEP 7: EXPECT RESULTS

If you sincerely humble yourself before the Lord, repent, pray and seek God's face; if you consistently meditate on His Word, you will experience a heightened awareness of His presence (John 14:21). The Lord will give you fresh, new spiritual insights. Your confidence and faith in God will be strengthened. You will feel mentally, spiritually, and physically refreshed. You will see answers to your prayers.

A single fast, however, is not a spiritual cure-all. Just as we need fresh infillings of the Holy Spirit daily, we also need new times of fasting before God. A 24-hour fast each week has been greatly rewarding to many Christians.

It takes time to build your spiritual fasting muscles. If you fail to make it through your first fast, do not be discouraged. You may have tried to fast too long the first time out, or you may need to strengthen your understanding and resolve. As soon as possible. Undertake another fast until you do succeed. God will honour you for your faithfulness.

I encourage you to join me in fasting and prayer again and again until we truly experience revival in our homes, our churches, our beloved nation, and throughout the world.

Chapter Eleven

HOW TO EXPERIENCE AND MAINTAIN PERSONAL REVIVAL

1. Ask the Holy Spirit to reveal any unconfessed sin in your life.
2. Seek forgiveness from all whom you have offended, and forgive all who have hurt you. Make restitution where God leads.
3. Examine your motives in every word and deed. Ask the Lord to search and cleanse your heart daily.
4. Ask the Holy Spirit to guard your walk against complacency and mediocrity.
5. Praise and give thanks to God continually in all ways on all days, regardless of your circumstances.
6. Refuse to obey your carnal (worldly) nature (Galatians 5:16,17).
7. Surrender your life to Jesus Christ as your Saviour and Lord. Develop utter dependence on Him with total submission and humility.
8. Study the attributes of God.
9. Hunger and thirst after righteousness (Matthew 5:6).

10. Love God with all of your heart, soul, and mind (Matthew 22:37).

11. Appropriate the continual fullness and control of the Holy Spirit by faith on the basis of God's command (Ephesians 5:18) and promise (1 John 5:14,15).

12. Read, study, meditate on, and memorize God's holy, inspired infallible Word daily (Colossians 3:16).

13. Pray without ceasing (1 Thessalonians 5:17).

14. Pray and sing in the Spirit (tongues) (Eph 5:18).

15. Fast and pray one 24-hour period each week.

16. Seek to share Christ daily as a way of life, give out tracts.

17. Determine to live a holy, Godly life of obedience and faith.

18. Start or join a home or Cell Group; Bible study group that emphasises revival and a holy life.

19. Join a local church, submitting to the eldership and their vision, as led by the Spirit.

20. Be faithful – in study of the Word, in prayer, in witnessing, in tithing and giving, in church attendance.

21. Be a doer of the Word and not just a hearer, only deceiving your own self (James 1:22).

> **'Discipline'; that special ingredient needed to move from the reality of today to your dreams of tomorrow.**

Remember, **"God wants to do something in you, so He can do something through you."**

CHAPTER TWELVE

A CLARION CALL

I believe there is a 'clarion call' to the Christian church going out in the Spirit right now. It's midnight! God is calling His church to prayer and fasting! A 'clarion call', is a strongly expressed demand or request for action. It is Harvest Time!

It is the time or season for the greater glory to manifest in the land.

> *"According to the word that I covenanted with you when ye came out of Egypt, so my spirit remaineth among you: fear ye not. For thus saith the Lord of hosts; Yet once, it is a little while, and I will shake the heavens, and the earth, and the sea, and the dry land; And I will shake all nations, and the desire of all nations shall come: and I will fill this house with glory, saith the Lord of hosts. The silver is mine, and*

the gold is mine, saith the Lord of hosts. The glory of this latter house shall be greater than of the former, saith the Lord of hosts: and in this place will I give peace, saith the Lord of hosts" (Haggai 2:5-9).

We can see from these verses that the Lord is speaking here of a time when He is going to shake all nations and the desire of all nations will come to God. He the Lord, desires souls! You are the desire of His heart, Jesus died for the whole world. He gave His life for the pearls of great price. His blood purchased redemption for all people.

The Word says that when one finds a pearl of great price in a field, he purchases the entire field to obtain that pearl of great price.

We were redeemed with precious blood, divine blood, the blood of God (Acts 20:28). The blood of our Lord Jesus Christ was poured out to cleanse the sins of the entire world. Jesus said, "In my Father's house are many mansions, behold I go to prepare a place for you" (John 14:2).

The Father wants a full house. He is not willing that any should perish but that all would come to repentance. (2 Peter 3:9).

He says here in Haggai that the silver and the gold is His. We are living in the days when God wants to do the great transfer of wealth from the wicked to the hands of the just. This wealth is to be used for end time evangelism and harvest.

"And thou say in thine heart, My power and the might of mine hand hath gotten me this wealth. But thou shalt remember the Lord thy God: for it is he that giveth thee power to get wealth, that he may establish his covenant which he sware unto thy fathers, as it is this day" (Deuteronomy 8:17-18).

God goes on to say that the glory of the latter house shall be greater than the former and in this place will He give peace. We are in the last years of the last days and God is calling His church to prayer and a fresh commitment to Himself and His Kingdom. The Lord wants to bring in the final great harvest and He needs YOU! He needs us His Church, for we are co-labourers together with God. In the beginning of the book of Haggai 1:1-14, we read,

"In the second year of Darius the king, in the sixth month, in the first day of the month, came the word of the Lord by Haggai the prophet unto Zerubbabel the son of Shealtiel, governor of Judah, and to Joshua the son of Josedech, the high priest, saying, Thus speaketh the Lord of hosts, saying, This people say, The time is not come, the time that the Lord's house should be built. Then came the word of the Lord by Haggai the prophet, saying, Is it time for you, O ye, to dwell in your cieled houses, and this house lie waste? Now therefore thus saith the Lord of hosts; Consider your ways. Ye have sown much, and bring in little; ye eat, but ye have not enough; ye drink, but

ye are not filled with drink; ye clothe you, but there is none warm; and he that earneth wages earneth wages to put it into a bag with holes. Thus saith the Lord of hosts; Consider your ways. Go up to the mountain, and bring wood, and build the house; and I will take pleasure in it, and I will be glorified, saith the Lord. Ye looked for much, and, lo it came to little; and when ye brought it home, I did blow upon it. Why? saith the Lord of hosts. Because of mine house that is waste, and ye run every man unto his own house. Therefore the heaven over you is stayed from dew, and the earth is stayed from her fruit. And I called for a drought upon the land, and upon the mountains, and upon the corn, and upon the new wine, and upon the oil, and upon that which the ground bringeth forth, and upon men, and upon cattle, and upon all the labour of the hands. Then Zerubbabel the son of Shealtiel, and Joshua the son of Josedech, the high priest, with all the remnant of the people, obeyed the voice of the Lord their God, and the words of Haggai the prophet, as the Lord their God had sent him, and the people did fear before the Lord. Then spake Haggai the Lord's messenger in the Lord's message unto the people, saying, I am with you, saith the Lord. And the Lord stirred up the spirit of Zerubbabel the son of Shealtiel, governor of Judah, and the spirit of Joshua the son of Josedech, the high priest, and the spirit of all the remnant of the people; and they came *and did work in the house of the Lord of hosts, their God"* (Haggai 1:1-14).

God told His people to consider their ways, as they obeyed the Lord and came and did work, building the house of the Lord. He took pleasure in it and was glorified in it. He was with them, as they turned to Him and He stirred them with His Spirit, giving them fresh energy and renewed youth to serve Him.

This resulted in the out-pouring of glory. God again is calling us to repentance and prayer, to come and do work in His house and build His Kingdom. God wants to do a work in you, so that He can do a work through you! God is in you for your benefit, but He is on you for who you come in contact with. God said to me, "Shaun, you've got to get what's in you, on you!"

The Kingdom of God is within you (Luke 17:21). We have the Holy Spirit, but God wants us filled to overflowing, with the Holy Spirit. Jesus told us, how much more will the Father give the Holy Spirit to those that ask (Luke 11:13). The Word also tells us in Ephesians 5:18, to stay filled with the Spirit of God.

Jesus spent hours, sometimes days in prayer. It was His habit to rise early and pray. **If we want something we have never had, we have to do something we have never done.**

Jesus said, while He was on the earth, "I must be about my Father's business" (Luke 2:49). These were the first recorded words of Jesus. This shows us the importance of the ministry that God has called us to. We are the body of Christ, we are filled with the Spirit of God and Jesus said, "My Father's house shall be called a house of prayer" (Matthew 21:13).

God's business is souls and it takes prayer, dedication and proclaiming the Word to win souls! We are called to be fishes to men! And we are called to prayer. Billye Brim, a prayer warrior who has ministered in our church, had conversations with David DuPlessis before he was promoted to glory. Plus a prophetic word given to evangelist Chris Harvey, a personal friend of mine, by prophet Bob Jones, are recorded below.

Here are Billye Brim's notes from her conversation, about what Smith Wigglesworth said concerning the last great revival before Jesus comes, starting in Australia and the surrounding South Pacific Islands.

> *"Now, regarding Wigglesworth. Here is how I remember what David DuPlessis shared with us about it.*
>
> *It happened in South Africa. David's father was pastor of a church where Wigglesworth was speaking. Wigglesworth had just come from Australia and the Islands there around. Young David was translating Wigglesworth into some local language as he preached.*
>
> *Very early one morning David was in his office when the door burst open and Wigglesworth stormed in. David stood. Wigglesworth took him by the clothing*

and pinned him to the wall. He prophesied concerning the moves of God that would take place before the Lord comes. He said there would be a great move of the Spirit in which classical denominational people would receive the baptism with the Holy Spirit. He said that he would not live to see this, but that David would and that God would use him among the denominational people. Especially, the Catholics.

(It is a little unclear to my memory, but I think it was here that I heard he said there would be a move of the Spirit and then a move of the Word and then a move of the Word and the Spirit together. After which the Lord would come. Now I know I have heard this part, but I am not sure I heard it from David.)

I did hear from David that Wigglesworth said the last great outpouring of the Holy Spirit before Jesus comes would be in Australia, New Zealand, and the islands.

David DuPlessis said that Wigglesworth after delivering the powerful prophecy let him go and left the room.

Later that morning they met the rest of the ministry team for breakfast. Wigglesworth said to David, "Good morning, David. Good to see you. How are you?" David said, "Brother Wigglesworth, you've already seen me this morning. But you didn't greet me." Wigglesworth replied, "This morning that was the man of God, on the way with the Word of God, greeting no man in the way. This is Wigglesworth. Good morning David."

WORD FROM BOB JONES TO CHRIS HARVEY
Sept 2009 Concerning Australian Awakening and the billion soul harvest, before Jesus returns.

"After receiving a word to go to the seer's house in South Carolina in September 2009, I finally obeyed God as I am not in the habit of breaking protocol and just turning up at somebody's residence, especially anointed servants of God.

We arrived at Bob's residence and he told his wife to let my wife and I in because he had been waiting for us. As we walked in I said, "I am an evangelist from Australia," his response was, "say no more. I already know that God told me you were coming. Sit down and I will do the talking."

The first words that Bob said were, "You are in the will of God in Australia stay there," because we had moved back there four and a half years earlier after living in the states for 10 years. He said, "Australia is spiritually asleep and God is about to wake her up." He said that, "We had been sent back to wake her up and we had nearly fallen asleep ourselves because of the apathy down-under." He said, "Your biggest enemy has not been the world, but divination through controlling leaders in the churches."

We had just previously been doing a conference at All Nations Church SC. The Pastor, Mahesh Chavda informed me that there had been a lot of angel activity around their church lately, and he had recently had a vision of an angel that was covered in red dust, which was bizarre because the day before we returned to Sydney was when the big red dust storm hit town.

In one of those meetings at All Nations Church, we had a powerful visitation of God's love, where everybody was weeping including myself. Just before this move of the Spirit, I felt something land behind me at the pulpit, it was sudden and frightening. It felt like a massive bird had landed behind me; I could not see anything, but felt the wind and the Presence. I thought it was an angel but knew in my spirit for some reason it was an eagle. It seemed to have a wingspan of 40 feet, which came to mind when it happened.

With no knowledge of myself and these meetings, Bob looked at me and said, "I have one question for you, how wide were the wings of that eagle that landed behind you at the pulpit on Rosh Hashanah?" (which is the spiritual new year for the Hebrews). I replied, "I wasn't sure, but it seemed like 40 feet." He looked at the other man in the room at the time and said, "See what I had told you before they came into the room?"

He said, "Do you realize what these two things mean?" "No", I said.
1. The number 40 speaks of one generation.
2. Rosh Hashanah date change has gone from 5769 to 5770.

Then he asked me, "Do you know what happened in 69' ?" I did not have a clue. "Woodstock, the Rock & Roll festival at Bethel New York" he replied. Then he said, "it has been 40 years since then until now, which is one generation," and he pointed to my wife and said, "That's your birthday, August 16th in Australia but August 15th in American because of the time change, the 15th of August 1969 was when Woodstock started, and a whole generation of people were lost out of that new mindset that came into the earth."

"But now, God is about to do a new thing. There is going to start a spiritual Woodstock in Australia." He never gave me a date or day but he said it will come and the church will not be ready for it. "The thrust of it will come out of free worship; it will go to the open fields because buildings will not be able to contain it, and at it's peak there will be <u>a thousand a day first time decisions.</u> It will spread from Brisbane through Sydney right around to Perth, then to New Zealand, England and the rest of the world." "And in this next generation there will be one billion souls saved in the western world through this awakening."

"This is the last great move of God spoken of by Smith Wigglesworth." Then he gave me 1 Cor 16:9, "For a great door and effectual is opened unto me, and there are many adversaries." I looked up the Greek and it meant a mega door of the Spirit.

I asked him how would this move of God take place because it was pretty tough in Australia, he said, "The Spirit of true repentance would come upon the nation and the Ministers would begin to weep uncontrollably, as their hearts were melted under the compassion of God. Just like what happened in that meeting on Rosh Hashanah at All Nations Church."

He said it would not happen straight away but God would use me and many others to prepare the way. He said it would get very dark in the world in this hour, but the church would shine like never before. He told me that I had fought many enemies. He surprised me by telling me that he'd only met five men in his 80 years, who had fought so many devils. He said, "It's a wonder you still have your mind!" Then he took me outside his house to pray for me. I said, "Why are you taking me outside?" He replied, "Because I am too old to fight whatever you've been fighting Down Under." I was instantly changed when he laid hands on me. My arms shot up to heaven, and my eyes were opened to a whole new level of spiritual insight. I could see enemies coming my way ahead of time.

Since then, we have done a 'forerunner spiritual tour' of Australia, which began in Pastor Shaun Marler's church, World Harvest, Brisbane, and went all the way around the coast to Perth, Western Australia. This 'Pour it Out Tour', saw that people were very responsive and encouraged by this word that was given. Many have sowed sacred seeds into this new move of God as a first fruits offering and we believe their prayers and giving have gone up as a memorial to God from the 'Great South Land of The Holy Spirit'."

Chris told me, when Bob Jones the prophet gave him the word about the Australian revival in 2009 that Chris asked him for a sign that the word was true. Bob Jones told Chris, "When you fly back to Australia from the USA, the day you land at the airport in Sydney, all the planes will be covered in red dust, the same colour as Uluru."

Chris said that he landed on the 22nd September 2009 and a strange phenomenon had happened. A pall of red dust had blown in from the outback and clogged the skies over Sydney on the Wednesday, diverting international flights and disrupting public transport. Also promoting a spike in emergency calls from people suffering breathing difficulties.

This cloud of red dust was so large, it went up the East Coast all the way into Queensland. The planes were covered in the red dust as the prophet had said, to confirm the spoken word.

Let's all push in together, let's all pray. Wherever we live in this wonderful world, let's fast and pray for the final great outpouring of the Holy Spirit to usher in the final great harvest of souls before Jesus comes, at the Rapture of the Church.

This harvest will take dedication, discipline, fasting, prayers and giving. It will require finances, God will raise up people to fund this last great harvest and transfer wealth to their hands. Jesus said the fields are white for harvest, but the labourers are few (Matthew 9:37). Will you join with me and be one to labour in this last great harvest for the Kingdom of God?

Revival Proclaimed by God!

The Lord told us in the book of Hosea 6:2,

> *"After two days He will revive us: in the third day He will raise us up, and we shall live in his sight."*

We are at the end of the Church Age, the two days of grace or the last two thousand years of history. We are at the beginning of the third day which will be the one thousand year or one day reign of Jesus Christ known as His Millennial Reign.

In this season of time, between the end of the second day and the beginning of the third the Lord has said, "He will revive us!" Let's together call for this last great outpouring, "The Greater Glory", which will usher in the greatest harvest of souls the world has ever seen.

"Say not ye, There are yet four months, and then cometh harvest? behold, I say unto you, Lift up your eyes, and look on the fields; for they are white already to harvest" (John 4:35).

"But ye shall receive power, after that the Holy Ghost is come upon you: and ye shall be witnesses unto me both in Jerusalem, and in all Judaea, and in Samaria, and unto the uttermost part of the earth" (Acts 1:8).

Our Response

"O Lord, I have heard Your speech, and was afraid: O Lord, revive Your work in the midst of the years, in the midst of the years make known; in wrath remember mercy" (Habakkuk 3:2).

Father, fill us with the Holy Spirit, in Jesus name and use us for your glory!

A final word from the author...

JESUS LOVES YOU

"The thief comes only to steal and kill and destroy; I have come that they may have life, and have it to the full" (John 10:10 NIV).

You are very special. GOD LOVES YOU. He sent His son Jesus Christ who died for you and was raised from the dead, that you might have an abundant life of victory in Him. You are a somebody because you were created by God and He doesn't make nobodies.

Your are God's best, His dream, His idea. You were created for a purpose and God has great and wonderful things in store for your life.

"For I know the plans I have for you," declares the Lord, "plans to prosper you and not to harm you, plans to give you hope and a future. Then you will call upon me and come and pray to me, and I will listen to you. You will seek me and find me when you seek me with all your heart. I will be found by you, declares the Lord..." (Jeremiah 29:11-14 NIV).

WHAT DOES GOD SAY?

ROMANS 3:23 "For all have sinned and fall short of the glory of God."

ROMANS 6:23 "The wages of sin is death, but the gift of God is eternal life in Christ Jesus our Lord."

JOHN 3:16 "For God so loved the world that He gave His only begotten Son, that whosoever believes in Him should not perish but have everlasting life."

ACTS 4:12 "Nor is there salvation in any other name under heaven given among men by which we must be saved."

TITUS 3:5 "Not by works of righteousness which we have done, but according to His mercy He saved us…"

1 JOHN 1:9 "If we confess our sins He is faithful and just to forgive us our sins and cleanse us from all unrighteousness."

2 CORINTHIANS 5:21 "For He made Him who knew no sin to be sin for us, that we might become the righteousness of God in Him."

ROMANS 10:9-10 "That if you confess with your mouth the Lord Jesus and believe in your heart that God has raised Him from the dead, you will be saved. For with the heart one believes unto righteousness, and with the mouth confession is made unto salvation."

SALVATION PRAYER

Heavenly Father, I thank you that you sent your Son, Jesus, to die on the cross for me. I repent of all my sins, and ask for your forgiveness.

Jesus come into my heart, in the person and presence of your Holy Spirit and be my personal Lord and Saviour. I believe with my heart and I confess with my mouth that Jesus Christ is Lord. Father, baptise me with your Holy Spirit and change me into the kind of person you want me to be.

I am now a Child of Almighty God. Thank you for saving me. In Jesus name, Amen.

APPENDIX

As I was reading over my final draft of this book I felt impressed of the Lord to include some further prophecies that have been given in the last hundred years or so by notable men and women of God concerning what God wants to do in these last days through a great end-time revival that will result in a massive harvest of souls before Jesus comes at the Rapture of the Church.

A scripture that God quickened to me concerning this outpouring of His Spirit in these days was Zach 10:1.

> *"Ask ye of the Lord rain in the time of the latter rain; so the Lord shall make bright clouds, and give them showers of rain, to every one grass in the field"* (Zechariah 10:1).

We know from Joel's prophecy that God said, "In the last days it will come to pass that He will pour out His Spirit on all flesh," I believe we can see from the above scripture that we have a responsibility to ask God for this great out pouring in these last days in which we live.

The following are other prophetic words by former great generals of God that declared these outpourings for our time.

TOMMY HICKS VISION
July 25, 1961

"My message begins, July 25th, about 2.30 in the morning, at Winnipeg, Canada. I had hardly fallen asleep when the vision and the revelation that God gave to me came before me. The vision came three times, exactly in detail, the morning of July 25th, 1961. I was so stirred and so moved by the revelation, that this has changed my complete outlook upon the Body of Christ, and upon the last end-time ministry. The greatest thing that the Church of Jesus Christ - that has ever been given to the Church -lies straight ahead. It is so hard to help men and women to realize and understand the thing that God is trying to give to His people in the end-time.

As the vision appeared to me, after I was asleep, I suddenly found myself at a great high distance. Where I was, I do not know, but as I was looking down upon the earth - suddenly the whole earth came into view - every nation, every kindred, every tongue came before my sight. From the east and from the west; from the north and the south; and I recognized every country, and many cities that I had been in. And I was almost in fear and trembling as I beheld the sight before me. And at that moment, as the earth came into view, it began to lightning and thunder. As the lightning flashed over the face of the earth, my eyes went downwards. I was facing the north. Suddenly I beheld what looked like a giant - and as I stared and looked at it, I was almost bewildered by the sight. It was so gigantic and so great in stature; his feet seemed to reach to the North Pole and his head to the south; its arms were stretched from sea to sea. I could not even begin to understand whether this was a mountain or whether this be a giant. But as I watched it, I suddenly beheld this great giant, I could see it was struggling for life, to even live. But his body was covered with debris from head to foot; and at times this great giant would move its body and act as though it would even rise up at times. And when it did, thousands of little creatures seemed to run away - hideous looking creatures would run away from this giant - and when he would become calm, they would come back.

All of a sudden this great giant lifted his hand toward the heavens, and then it lifted its other hand; and when it did, these creatures by the thousands seemed to flee way from this giant and go into the darkness, and into the night.

Slowly this great giant began to rise - and as he did, his head and hands went into the clouds. As he arose to his feet he seemed to have cleansed himself from the debris and filth that was upon him, and he began to raise his hands into the heavens as though praising the Lord. And as he raised his hands it was even unto the clouds.

Suddenly, every cloud became silver. The most beautiful silver that I have ever known. As I watched this phenomena, it was so great, I could not even begin to understand what it all meant. I was so stirred as I watched it and cried unto the Lord, and I said, 'Oh, Lord, what is the meaning of this?' And it felt as if I was actually in the Spirit and I could feel the presence of the Lord, even as I was asleep.

And from the clouds, suddenly, there came great drops of liquid light raining down upon the mighty giant, and slowly, slowly, this giant began to melt; began to sink, as it were, into the very earth itself. And as he melted, his whole form seemed to have melted upon the face of the earth. And this great rain began to come down; liquid drops of light, as it were, began to flood the very earth itself. And as I watched this giant that seemed to melt, suddenly it became millions of people over the face of the earth. As I beheld the sight before me, people stood up all over the world. They were lifting their hands and they were praising the Lord.

At that very moment there came a great thunder that seemed to roar from the heavens.

I turned my eyes toward the heavens and suddenly I saw a figure in white – glistening white - the most glorious thing I have ever seen in all my life. I did not see the face, but somehow I knew that it was the Lord Jesus Christ. And as He stretched forth His hand - as He did - He would stretch forth His hand upon the peoples and the nations of the world, men and women. As He pointed towards them, this liquid light seemed to flow from His hand into this person and a mighty anointing of God came upon them. And those people began to go forth in the Name of the Lord.

I do not know how long I watched. It seemed it went into days and weeks and months, and I beheld Christ as He continued to stretch forth His hand. But there was a tragedy. There were many people, as He stretched forth His hand, that refused the anointing of God, and the call of God. I saw men and women that I knew, people that I felt that certainly they would receive the call of God, but as He stretched forth His hand toward this one, and toward that one, they simply bowed their heads and began to back away.

And to each of those who seemed to bow down and back away, they seemed to go into darkness. Blackness seemed to swallow them everywhere.

I was bewildered as I watched it. But these people that He had anointed - hundreds of thousands of people all over the world - in Africa, Asia, Russia, China, America - all over the world - the anointing of God was upon these people as they went forth in the Name of the Lord. I saw these men and women as they went forth. They were ditch diggers; they were washerwomen; they were rich men; they were poor men. I saw people who were bound with paralysis and sickness, and blindness and deafness. As the Lord stretched forth His hand to give them the anointing, they became well; they became healed, and they went forth.

And this is the miracle of it. This is the glorious miracle of it; those people would stretch forth their hand exactly as the Lord did, and it seemed that there was this same liquid fire that seemed to be in their hand; as they stretched forth their hand they said, 'According to my word, be thou made whole.'

As these people continued in this mighty end-time ministry, I did not fully realize what it was. And I looked to the Lord and said, 'What is the meaning of this?' And He said, 'This is that, that I will do in the last days. I will restore all that the cankerworm, the palmerworm, the caterpillar - I will restore all that they have destroyed. 'This, My people in the end-time, shall go forth; as a mighty army they will sweep over the face of the earth.'

As I was at a great height, I watched these people as they were going to and fro over the face of the earth. Suddenly there was a man in Africa, and in a moment he was transported in the Spirit of God, and perhaps he was in Russia, or China, or America, or some other place, and vice versa; all over the world these people went. And they came through fire and through pestilence and through famine. Neither fire nor persecution - nothing seemed to stop them.

Angry mobs came to them with swords and with guns, and like Jesus, they passed through the multitude and they could not find them. But they went forth in the Name of the Lord, and everywhere they stretched forth their hand the sick were healed, the blind eyes were opened. There was no long prayer.

And one of the things that seemed - after I had reviewed the vision so many times in my mind; and I thought about it so many times - I never saw a church, and I never saw or heard a denomination; but these people were going in the Name of the Lord of hosts. Hallelujah!

As they marched forward, everything they did as the ministry of Christ, in the end-time. These people were ministering to the multitudes over the face of the earth. Tens of thousands, even millions, seemed to come to the Lord Jesus Christ as these people stood forth and gave the message of the Kingdom - of a coming Kingdom - in this last hour. It was so glorious.

God is going to give to the world a demonstration in this last hour such as the world has never known. These men and women are of all walks of life. Degrees will mean nothing.

I saw these workers as they were going forth over the face of the earth. When one would seem to stumble and fall another would come and pick them up. There was no big 'I' and little 'You', but every mountain was brought low and every valley was exalted, and they seemed to have one thing in common; there was divine love that seemed to flow forth from these people as they went together, as they worked together, as they lived together. It was the most glorious thing that I have ever known. Jesus Christ was the theme of their life.

As I watched from the very heaven itself, there were times when great deluges of this liquid light seemed to fall upon great congregations. And that congregation would lift their hands and seemingly praise God for hours and even days as the Spirit of God came upon them. God said, 'I will pour My Spirit upon all flesh,' and that is exactly the thing that God was doing; and to every man and to every woman that received this power and the anointing of God; the miracles of God - there was no ending to it. And then again, as these people were going about the face of the earth, a great persecution seemed to come from every end of the earth.

Suddenly, there was another loud clap of thunder that seemed to resound around the world, and I heard, again, the voice. The voice seemed to speak, 'Now this is My people, this is My beloved bride.' And when the voice spoke, I looked upon the earth and I could see the lakes and the mountains. The graves were opened and people from all over the world; the saints of all ages seemed to be rising. As they rose from the graves, suddenly, all these people came from every direction, and they seemed to be forming again, this gigantic body. As the dead in Christ seemed to be rising first, I could hardly comprehend it. It was so marvelous; it was far beyond anything I could ever dream or think of.

But, as the body suddenly began to form and take shape again, it took shape again in the form of this mighty giant. But this time it was different. It was arrayed in the most beautiful, gorgeous white. It's garments were without spot or wrinkle as the body began to form. And the people of all ages seemed to be gathering into this body, and slowly, slowly, as it began to form up into the heavens, suddenly from the heavens above, the Lord Jesus came - became the Head. And I heard another clap of thunder that said, 'This is My beloved Bride in who I have waited. She will come forth, even tried by fire. This is she that I have loved from the beginning of time.'

As I watched, my eyes suddenly turned to the far north and I saw – seemingly destruction - men and women in anguish and crying out, and buildings in destruction. Then I heard again the fourth voice that said, 'Now is My wrath being poured forth upon the face of the earth.' From the ends of the whole world the wrath of God seemed to be poured out and it seemed that there were great vials of God's wrath being poured out upon the face of the earth. I can remember it as though it happened a moment ago. I shook and trembled as I beheld the awful sight of seeing cities, and whole nations, going down to destruction. I could hear the weeping and the wailing. I could hear people crying. They seemed to cry as they went into caves, but the caves and the mountains opened up. They leaped into water, but the water would not drown them. There was nothing that seemingly could destroy them. They were wanting to take their life but they could not take it.

Then again, I turned my eyes unto the Body, arrayed in the beautiful white garment. Slowly, slowly, it began to rise from the earth. As it did, I awoke. I had seen the end-time ministry; the last hour. Again on July 27, at 2.20 in the morning, the same revelation; the same vision, came exactly as it did before."

The 100-YEAR-OLD PROPHECY -Michael Edds

"The great Azusa Street Awakening, which over the years resulted in 600 million being swept into the Kingdom of God and gave birth to the Pentecostal Movement, began in 1906. It was one of the greatest outpourings of the Spirit of God since Pentecost. Multitudes were saved, healed, and filled with the Holy Spirit. Incredible miracles occurred.

This great revival moved from Los Angeles to its new focal point of Chicago, Illinois. The two great centers of revival in Chicago were the North Avenue Mission and the Stone Church. Pentecost swept from Chicago to Canada, Europe, South America and Africa. One of the greatest outpourings occurred at Stone Church in 1913. The renown evangelist Maria Woodworth Etter began a revival on July 2, 1913 at Stone Church.

The services were to last until the end of July but continued for six months. This was a time of divine appointment for the city of Chicago; God rent the heavens and came down!! Scenes from the days of the Early Church began to occur at Stone Church. Word began to spread throughout Chicago of miraculous healings, deliverance from demonic possession, conversions, and of the outpouring of the Holy Spirit happening in these meetings. Advertisement was no longer necessary! The city was incredibly shaken. Word spread of the miraculous intervention of God. Thousands came on trolleys, buggies, and trains, while many walked. Some came from distances of 1,600 miles away. 1200 to 1500 packed into Stone Church each night. The basement was filled and many stood out on the street. Street meetings were held to accommodate them. Three services were held on Sundays!

As Christians prayed around the altar one evening, Sister Woodworth-Etter and others gave the following powerful prophecy and divine promise, which they prophesied would occur within 100 years of the 1913 Chicago Visitation. She prophesied of this coming End Time Revival....

"We are not yet up to the fullness of the Former Rain and that when the Latter Rain comes, it will far exceed anything we have seen!" William Seymour, the leader of the Azusa Street Awakening, also prophesied that in 100 years there would be an outpouring of God's Spirit and His Shekinah Glory that would be greater and more far reaching than what was experienced at Azusa. It has been almost 100 years since these prophecies were given... I believe that we have reached the time of the fulfillment of these 100 year old prophecies. We must be diligent to pray, intercede and protect what the Lord is doing. We must encourage and edify one another as never before. We must crucify every critical, judgmental and religious spirit that may be within us. We must put on the holiness and righteousness of Christ. Our time of divine destiny has come. We are about to experience what Brother Seymour and Sister Woodworth-Etter foresaw. God is about to rend the heavens and come down!...

The Last Revival Prophecy by Smith Wigglesworth's Before He Passed on to Glory.

It shall come to pass afterward that I will pour out My Spirit on all flesh; Your sons and your daughters shall prophesy, Your old men shall dream dreams, Your young men shall see visions– Joel 2:28.

Smith Wigglesworth (1859-1947), known as the apostle of faith, moved in mighty signs and wonders, and even raised people from the dead! Shortly before he passed into glory he prophesied, "During the next few decades there will be two distinct moves of the Holy Spirit across the Church in Great Britain. The first move will affect every church that is open to receive it and will be characterised by the restoration of the baptism and gifts of the Holy Spirit.

"The second move of the Holy Spirit will result in people leaving historic churches and planting new churches. In the duration of each of these moves, the people who are involved will say, 'This is a great revival.' But the Lord says, 'No, neither is this the great revival but both are steps towards it.'

"When the new church phase is on the wane, there will be evidence in the churches of something that has not been seen before: a coming together of those with an emphasis on the Word and those with an emphasis on the Spirit.

"When the Word and the Spirit come together, there will be the biggest move of the Holy Spirit that the nations, and indeed, the world have ever seen. It will mark the beginning of a revival that will eclipse anything that has been witnessed within these shores, even the Wesleyan and Welsh revivals of former years.

"The outpouring of God's Spirit will flow over from the United Kingdom to mainland Europe, and from there, will begin a missionary move to the ends of the earth."

The Promised Revival

William Seymour, known as the leader of the Azusa Street Revival, released a prophecy in 1909 as the revival was starting to wane. He declared that in about 100 years there would come another move of God that would make the Azusa Revival pale in comparison. This was quite a declaration from a man who had experienced the shekinah glory of God, saw limbs grow back, tumors fall off, and countless people sent to the nations as carriers of the glory that God manifested there in Los Angeles at the turn of the century.

As stated previously, I felt impressed of the Lord to include these prophecies in this book. Jesus said,

> *"And Jesus came and spake unto them, saying, All power is given unto me in heaven and in earth. Go ye therefore, and teach all nations, baptizing them in the name of the Father, and of the Son, and of the Holy Ghost: Teaching them to observe all things whatsoever I have commanded you: and, lo, I am with you always, even unto the end of the world. Amen"* (Matthew 28:18-20).

It is interesting to note that Chris Harvey received the prophecy from Bob Jones in 2009, which is 100 years after the William Seymour prophecy. In Acts 1:8 Jesus said,

> *"But ye shall receive power, after that the Holy Ghost is come upon you: and ye shall be witnesses unto me both in Jerusalem, and in all Judaea, and in Samaria, and unto the uttermost part of the earth"* (Acts 1:8).

I believe that with all my heart we are living in the days when God wants to pour out His Spirit upon all flesh, resulting in a huge harvest of souls for the glory of God! I have written this book and now have included these prophecies, to inspire and encourage us all to believe to see, "the glory of God" manifest upon all the nations of the world. Remember in Isaiah it says, "the glory of God shall be seen upon you the people of God." It is also says in Habakkuk 2:14, "that the whole earth shall be filled with the knowledge of the glory of God as the waters cover the sea."

Together, let us love more, reach more, win more and do more for Jesus!

Footnotes

The following is a list of resources and sources, read and studied in the preparation of this book. Plus, further thankyous and acknowledgements to individuals who have had an impact on my life. Their thoughts, prayers and inspiration (some of which I have included in this work) have helped mould me, enlighten my thinking and inspired me to grow and touch this world for Christ.

King James Bible.
Amplified Bible. Jointly published by Zondervan and The Lockman Foundation.
NIV Bible. Published by Zondervan in the United States and Hodder & Stoughton in the UK.
Strong's Concordance. Published by Thomas Nelson Publishers.
Dake Annotated Reference Bible. Published by Dake's Publishing Inc.
Bible Hub. biblehub.com
Google Dictionary.
Prayer and Fasting by Gordon Lindsay.
Fasting Schedules by Dr. Julio C. Ruibal.
Fasting by Drummond Thom.
How to Fast Successfully by Derek Prince, Whitaker House.
Chris Harvey for supplying Bob Jones's prophecy.
Personal conversations with Don Gossett.
Billye Brim's notes on conversations with David DuPlessis, a South African Pentecostal Minister, considered as one of the Founders of the Charismatic Movement, that spread world-wide. Who was affectionately known as 'Mr. Pentecost'.
Evangelist Steve Ryder for his mentor-ship in my earlier ministry and his commitment to see revival and God's miracle healing power manifest throughout Australia and the world!

Also by Dr. Shaun Marler

The Rapture of the Church
This book will help you prepare for the next great event on the Christian calendar. Learn what the word 'Rapture' means -God's ability to catch up people alive to His presence. Timelines included, pointing to when we can expect this event to occur and much more!

Life Changing Principles For Victorious Living
Life Changing Principles for Victorious Living is a must read! You will find keys to unlock your life in Christ.

Praise Power
Everything in your life is subject to change. God's will for your life is that it changes for the better. How do you get there? Through praise in the Word, because praise is the verbal expression of Faith and Faith is the language of Heaven.

Divine Healing 101
This is a how-to book with examples, teachings and personal testimonies, that prove it is God's will that you not only be healed, but walk in divine health, all the days of your life.

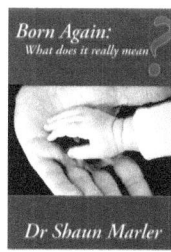

Born Again; What does it really mean?
This mini book is a must have! You will learn how you can accept Jesus Christ as Saviour and what it really means to be born again. Discover how you can enjoy all the blessings will now belong to you!

These books and other titles are available on Amazon as well as other online bookstores around the world!

PARTNERSHIP

Help Pastor Shaun to help others, by becoming a Harvest Partner in this great work of spreading the gospel and loving others.

Please email general@whm.org.au and become a World Harvest partner today!

For other information and a complete list of products, or to find out how you can partner with the ministry of Dr Shaun Marler and World Harvest Ministries, contact:
P.O. Box 90, Bald Hills, 4036
Queensland, Australia
Phone: +61 7 3261 4555
(9am – 4:30pm EST Aust)

Web: whm.org.au
Email: general@whm.org.au

Facebook: www.facebook.com/worldharvestmin
Facebook: www.facebook.com/ShaunMarlerWHM
Twitter: twitter.com/world_harvest
Youtube: youtube.com/worldharvestlife
Instagram: @i_harvest

Natural Superfoods is partnering with World Harvest Ministries. 10% of their income goes to support our mission programs, helping to feed widows, orphans and reaching the lost for Christ.

Natural Superfoods and Co have great products for detoxing and helping people maintain optimum health. These products, like their "Enlighten Supergreens", which are a unique proprietary blend of powerful, natural, organic superfoods, designed to boost your immune system, can be used while fasting and also are great as a daily supplement for general well-being.

If you desire to purchase any of these amazing supplements, you can do so by visiting their domain:

naturalsuperfoodsco.com

Raw plant based superfoods to support balanced healthy living.

10% of your purchase will go to supporting the ministry. In this way, your own health can benefit at the same time you will be helping us to help others.

**'Discipline'; just one word
but a powerful ingredient to
achieve life's targets.**

Be blessed, and successful fasting!
Ps. Shaun.

NOTES

I have added a few blank pages here for you to write down your own thoughts, inspirations and revelations from our Lord, as you read, study and meditate the scriptures in this book. What you learn, what you glean, teach others that they too may grow in the Lord and become very effective in life and ministry. I leave you with one last scripture.

Beloved, I wish above all things that thou mayest prosper and be in health, even as thy soul prospereth.
3 John 2

NOTES

NOTES

NOTES

ABOUT THE AUTHOR

Dr Shaun Marler is the Senior Pastor and co-founder with his wife Kerrie of World Harvest Ministries, an international organisation based in Queensland, Australia, World Harvest Ministries is committed to carrying out the Great Commission of Jesus our Lord. Taking the healing word to the nations and feeding the hungry, visiting prisoners, clothing the naked, visiting the widows and orphans in their affliction, and preaching the Good News to the poor.

World Harvest Ministries currently has programs in Australia, Africa and India, where the poor and destitute are given free medical treatment, orphan homes where children are fed, accommodated and educated, a ministry to widows who have been abandoned by society and a program to feed people with leprosy.

A portion of the proceeds of the sale of this book goes towards this valuable work, which is making a huge difference in the lives of others!

THE FAST WAY TO POWER

www.ingramcontent.com/pod-product-compliance
Lightning Source LLC
Chambersburg PA
CBHW031246290426
44109CB00012B/462